UNNATURAL ACTS

UNNATURAL ACTS

SUSAN SHELLOGG

⊰ B A R R I C A D E B O O K S ⊱
NEW YORK

Published by Barricade Books Inc.
61 Fourth Avenue
New York, NY 10003

Copyright © 1994 by Susan Shellogg

Printed in the United States of America.

Library of Congress Cataloging-in-Publication Data

Shellogg, Susan.
Unnatural acts/Susan Shellogg.
p. cm.
ISBN 1-56980-000-6: $21.00
1. Sadomasochism—New York (N.Y.)—Case studies. 2. Shellogg, Susan.
3. Prostitutes—New York (N.Y.)—Biography. I. Title.
HQ79.S53 1994
306.77'5—dc20   93-43563
                                                   CIP

First printing

FOR JOANIE

PHOTOGRAPH BY EDWARD TARR, 1941

ACKNOWLEDGMENTS

Thanks to Alvin, who introduced me to Carole and Lyle, who believed in me from the start, to Gil for his special talents, to Teri M. and to Ron.

If it hadn't been raining that night, I might not have become a professional dominatrix. I can see the weather report in my brain, a sort of personal meteorology: CLEAR SKIES, GO HOME AND WATCH LETTERMAN; RAIN, BECOME A DOMINATRIX.

But it did rain. It began to pour soon after we entered the Robert Miller Gallery, and I could see sheets of water washing clean the sealed windows of the chic, understated art space.

We had planned to stop in briefly at the opening, an exhibition of David Salle's erotic black-and-white photographs, and then proceed downtown to some clubs. The October downpour derailed those plans.

Every cab that went by had its top light off, and the poor souls who scurried by on the sidewalks were getting drenched. People huddled outside under the gallery awning, vainly trying to hail taxis.

A Travis Bickle rain, a friend of mine used to call it, after the character in *Taxi Driver*. *Some day a real rain is going to come down and wash the scum off the streets.* I looked out moodily onto the high-priced precincts of 57th Street.

I was in my club clothes: Claude Montana black leather pants, Armani tuxedo jacket with just naked flesh underneath. I had on a new pair of Charles Jourdans and I didn't want to ruin them, or show up at Nell's looking like a drowned rat.

I decided to stay at least until the rain lessened. The Salle exhibit was made up of photographs of people, women mostly, parading in black leather.

A lot of close-ups. Gynecological, or proctologic, as the case may be, in their detail. I noticed that the subject matter made all the men at the opening eager, as if every woman present had given her tacit approval to the act of sexual intercourse.

This might be what hell is like, I thought, locked in the Robert Miller gallery waiting for the rain to stop, surrounded by wall after wall of fuck-swollen genitalia.

Who had gotten me into this? Men, as usual.

Three men, to be exact. One was my good friend Alex, a Russian madman straight out of the mold of Raskolnikov and Rasputin and all those dragoons who volunteered for night watch in Catherine the Great's private quarters. He kept his craziness under wraps most of the time, so a lot of people knew him as a Russian Jay Gatsby, ambitious, successful at his chosen profession (a wholesale pot dealer) and something of a cipher. A cipher with a very beautiful heart.

We had met earlier at his Lower East Side loft, Alex and two of his friends. There was Alexander Danel, the sculptor—although I'm not sure he warrants the definite article, and perhaps he is just "a sculptor." And there was a man I had met before but had to be reintroduced to, Horst, older than the rest of us, 58, a leather designer.

The three men were dressed all in black, as I was, and looked fashionably unhealthy, which I didn't, having just returned from a wallet-busting junket to St. Bart's. In fact, I was throwing a sun-burnished glow off my skin that made me feel like a million bucks. This was back in the 80s, before a deep tan was considered a mark of folly.

The rest of them did cocaine while we gossiped and psyched ourselves for the death-march of fun that stretched ahead. I refrained. From the drug, I mean, not the gossip. I never saw the sense of cocaine, even other people's cocaine (which, as Mick Jagger points out, is a very different drug from your own cocaine).

Marijuana was my drug of choice, and that evening I stoked my engines on a jet-stick of Alex's exquisite varietal exotics.

"Teaheads are unfathomable to me," William S. Burroughs said once, at another party, in another life. Yes, we are, I replied to myself.

Half-loaded, ignoring the darkening skies, we piled four to a cab (we stuck Horst in front with the driver) to go uptown to Robert Miller. Alexander spoke vaguely of meeting a dealer there who might be interested in including some of his work in a show. It didn't matter. Manhattan is a place of whims connected by cab rides.

"What's at the gallery?" Horst asked, twisting around from the front seat.

"Pricks and pussies," Alexander said.

"But what about the art?" I asked, and the rest of them laughed.

Big, nickel-sized raindrops stained the sidewalk in front as we went inside. The crowd was an accordion mix of Uptown and Downtown, as if someone was playing origami with the map of Manhattan, and had folded the Village into Midtown.

"Let me take you to the cash bar," Alex muttered in his best Charles Boyer voice, and then he promptly disappeared. I took a tour, looked out at the rain, and soldiered through the assholians alone.

In the midst of all this I met Willie.

I am a sucker for Eurotrash. It's a handicap, I know, a behavioral quirk I've tried but haven't been able to correct.

Willie was Swiss Italian, with smooth, silvery hair, just hitting his apogee at 50, the age when most women hit the wall. Standing there in the New York gallery, he was a study in suave hipness, a boulevardier, a soigné sort of guy, with a thrusting, insistent style that bordered on campiness.

"How do you like the show?"

As a conversational gambit, not the most imaginative, but the way it just sits there on the page does not do justice to the way Willie said it. He had a rolling, European accent, which was killer for American women like me. If you recorded it and played it backwards, you'd get a number for a Swiss bank account.

How did I like the show? What was I going to say? Well, I think the leather-trussed cock over there has a certain elemental vivacity, but all the quivering, spit-slick labia were a bit too much, didn't he think?

He had hooded, icy-blue eyes, which were part of the requisite genetic baggage for all of these guys, as if God lost his marbles playing peery with them. They were piercing, unsettling. Only now they had decided to settle permanently on my breasts, to see if maybe they could pierce those. Thank God for a St. Bart's tan, which was my only armor.

And then something in those eyes triggered a jolt of recognition. It was a certain look Willie was giving me, the same look I had been getting from a certain class of men my whole adult life. It was a pleading, imploring, begging, whining look. I had even informally given it upper-case status—the Look—since I had seen it so often.

I already knew how I reacted to the Look. It made me want to hurt the purveyor of it, viciously and deeply. I don't think I'm alone in this. I think it's some innate human response to weakness and need.

If it hadn't been raining, if I hadn't been caught there, if Alex and Alexander and Horst hadn't jettisoned me, the night might have been different. I would have left the gallery already, or I would have dismissed this all-too-familiar Look in Willie's eyes as just one more sick missive from an overflowing mailbag.

He was mentioning Milan—of course, it would have to be Milan—and a family that had been in the textile business since the 1400s. When the Black Plague still roamed the earth, this man's ancestors were hacking down flax and weaving it into linen. Probably did a bang-up business in burial shrouds.

"What is your name, my dear?" Again, on the page, it is diminished. From his lips, though, the words took on an insinuating quality, arrogant and bold. It was as if he had asked me my innermost secrets.

"Sonya," I said, grabbing a nom de guerre that I had used once or twice before, when I didn't want to let a man get too close too fast. I spelled it for him.

"Sonya," he repeated, purring. He talked some more, and I felt somewhat swayed by his charm and at the same time outside of it, as if I were watching myself. I was a self-consciously hip American woman revealing her true innocence in conversation with the Continent. How very Jamesian.

And there was always the Look. I think that's really what did it for me. Because no matter how impressive and suave Willie was in conversation, the Look established our true dynamic. In one world, Willie was rich, polished, immune. In the other world, he was at my feet and I was the one triumphant. The two realities shifted beneath each other, sending off sparks of sexual friction.

I have since thought that this is a prescription for good, or at least interesting sex: to gain this textured level of role-playing. The Chinese box effect of sexual power. Outside the

bedroom, he's dominant, and she's the picture of subservience. Inside the bedroom, he's putty in milady's hands.

The rain had stopped and the gallery had cleared. "May I
buy you a drink?" Willie asked.

I did not see Alex or Alexander or Horst anywhere. Willie and
I were standing near the door, and anyone who left would have
had to go past us, but my three friends were nowhere in sight.

It didn't matter. Alex and I often went out together.
Implicit in our evenings on the town was that we were both
free agents, and one or the other of us had been swallowed
whole by nocturnal New York many times before this.

Willie and I walked out onto the puddled sidewalk,
standing for a moment without speaking, breathing in the
rain-freshened air.

With a confident, imperative gesture, he directed me to
Madison Avenue. We walked a short distance, around the
corner, Willie guiding, me allowing myself to be herded. I
guessed where he was taking me before we got there: La
Relais, a chic haunt of Europe trash.

I caught a look at myself in a wall panel of mirrors on the
way over there. Golden hair up in a French twist, dark tan,
black tux jacket with a generous display of cleavage, lipstick
and nails painted in the fresh red color of new blood.

I looked like a six-foot whore of Babylon.

If a sociologist or anthropologist is searching for a subject
to study, there is ample opportunity in the habits and
behavior of the modern-day European émigré in New York
City. It's such an incestuous little scene.

The young, monied habitués of Nell's, or Au Bar, or M.K. are almost grotesquely stylized. *Jeunesse dorée*, the French call them. Gilded youth. They all profess to despise America and Americans, but this loathing is so automatic that I suspect it's all somehow part of their armor of self-hatred. In spite of their professed disgust, they stay in New York anyway. They do not really regard it as part of America at all, but some cultural free-fire zone, an international city like Berlin or Hong Kong.

They never, never cross the Hudson, and they rarely stray from the sacred quadrant of the Upper East Side. They are insouciant about drug use and sex, and they view any limits placed on these activities as the height of bourgeois American morality, to be rejected and despised. They are implacably shallow.

La Relais was one of their haunts, and I saw a lot of tan young heads swivel when we walked in. In the endless calculation of prestige and money that goes on in their minds, they must have toted up Willie's Armani suit, and my whore of Babylon appearance, and concluded we were right where we belonged.

I once read of a hysterically devout medieval nun who dreamed about swallowing the foreskin of Christ, testifying that it went down her throat like liquid gold, and as I drank the first Stoli martini that evening, I think I knew how she felt. Ah, Vitamin V. It'll be the death of me yet.

I kept telling myself that I ought to get away, that this was not my scene, that the preening European cock-of-the-walk at my elbow cut a ridiculous figure. But Willie kept pulling me back in with his soothing voice and his good sense of humor. He was witty, clever, decadent. He told me stories about some of the young punks present, who their fathers were, where the families stole their money.

It was only when he turned his conversation to me that the clichés started to clang like brass spittoons. "You look like such a German," he said, which was, I suppose, his idea of a compliment. "I watched you across the gallery, and I was really very surprised when you turned out to be American. You are so statuesque." Clang!

I told him about a bronze that Alexander D. had done of me, a full body nude that had been literally purchased out of the foundry by a collector who had caught sight of it by chance. "Nude" and "bronze" were words that made Willie's eyes blaze like a couple of klieg lights. He was staring at my breasts like he wanted to crawl in between them and set up housekeeping.

Willie was devoted to opera (clang!), particularly Wagnerian opera (clang! clang!). "You remind me of a Rhinemaiden," he said (clang!), at which point all the Europunks in the bar stood up and applauded the audacious banality of his seduction technique.

It didn't matter. By the time I downed my third foreskin it seemed perfectly natural that I would go with Willie to his townhouse.

I expected to make out in the cab on the way up, but Willie merely leaned back in the seat and stared at me, the Look gleaming in his eyes like a fever.

"If you liked the photographs at the gallery," he said, "I think you'll like my place." Willie really knew how to fill a woman with delight and anticipation.

At another point in the short, five-block ride (short in distance, that is—in time it was longer, Manhattan being one of the only cities in the world which has traffic jams at midnight), Willie murmured, apropos of nothing, "You could do some real damage to me." Like I said, delight and anticipation.

With only Christ's foreskin and St. Bart's to protect me, I exited the cab with a man I had met only hours previously.

Willie lived in a high-priced spread in the East 60's. Stanford White, he told me. As we mounted his steps he explained that he was having a hard time getting the facade changed, because of the landmark status of the place. What he didn't explain was why anyone would want to change the facade of a Stanford White brownstone in the first place.

"It's a real pain, your American bureaucracy," he said. As opposed to the famously painless European variety.

When he unbolted the door, it swung open into a darkened interior. He snapped on a single small lamp. There were stairs to the right, and a pair of heavy sliding wooden doors to the left.

These we went through, to a room that was also rather dimly lit, its windows leaded with stained glass, illuminated only by the small, frame-mounted lights above a pair of paintings.

I still get a little shiver when I think of them. They immediately cleared my head of all the vodka I had been belting down. Both paintings were the same size, small, about a foot-

and-a-half square, hung in gilt frames on the interior wall. Matisses, from his south of France period.

Once upon a time I had styled myself an art student, and Matisse was one of my favorites, and the south of France my favorite of Matisse. I approached the paintings with reverence, resisting the impulse to ask if they were real.

Willie was across the room, busying himself with a couple of huge balloon brandy snifters. I examined each Matisse in turn, slowly, attempting to be languid about it. I wondered at the impossible luxury of actually living with such objects. Nothing clanged about the paintings at all.

The two oils made me feel small. Yes, I remembered, I really was an artist once. But that was in another country, and besides, the wench is dead. I had to think for a moment to recall just exactly where my paints and canvases were stored in my apartment.

I knew Willie had money from the moment I turned to find him at my elbow at the gallery. The Matisses confirmed a certain level of wealth that was rare and beyond my expectations.

"Rich," or "wealthy"—one term was supposed to be gauche, and one acceptable, but I was always forgetting which was which. "You must be very rich," I said, choosing wrong.

Willie smiled and squinted at me from the across the room. For the first time I thought he might be myopic, in which case perhaps the Matisses were wasted on him.

"Before the war, my family had real wealth," he said. "My grandfather had a lot of money that the fascists took."

He gave me a glass balloon roughly the size of the Goodyear blimp, with a little amber-colored Napoleon sloshing around in the bottom of it.

"I'd like to show you around downstairs," he said, the Look beaming out of his eyes like a search probe.

Down we went, taking the back stairs, into a muffled silence that indicated good sound-proofing at work. Total silence anywhere has always chilled me a bit, ever since I was a little girl, but silence in the middle of Manhattan was so odd as to be surreal. The sirens of the city faded and we were swallowed by Willie's madness.

The room he led me into was decorated in a style that skipped lightly across epochs and influences, but settled mostly upon Spain of the Inquisition and Victorian England of the late-brothel period. Black and red was the color theme. The floor was black marble, and there were several strategically placed mirrors throwing the interior back at itself.

The room was filled with the accouterments of sadomasochism. Elaborate devices of torture. A large rack on one wall, a whole other wall of costumes—capes, masks, hoods, gloves, breeches—and a third wall of implements.

This last was the most lurid, consisting of multiple hooks hung with gleaming catheters, nozzles, handcuffs, tongs and clamps, set off by shiny leather whips, crops and a huge cat-o-nine-tails. Two suspension devices dangled from the ceiling, one very elaborate and a simple one looking oddly like a pull-up bar from a high school gymnasium.

Willie's only comment while we were in his personal, private dungeon came when he fingered some of the hoses that hung on the wall. "When I was a young man in Amsterdam, after the war, a nurse taught me how to use these," he said. I nodded; I didn't know quite how one should respond to that.

I was still a little drunk, and the room seemed claustrophobic to me, but the reality of it was quite removed from what it would have been if I were sober. "Ooooh, what is all this shit?" I remember thinking vaguely, impressed more by the extent of it, the completeness of Willie's preparation, than by what it all meant.

Wordlessly, we went back upstairs. I had the feeling that Willie had opened a door into the dark room of his psyche, flicked on a flashlight, given me a quick glimpse, and then shut if off again.

Willie refilled his cognac balloon; I had barely tasted mine, but the fumes were doing the trick anyway. I sat down so I could face the genius of Matisse. I noticed there were other paintings and objets in the room; two murals, one of Athena and one of, yes, Brunhild. I brooded upon the unattractiveness, really, of the Brunhild archetype. A woman with horns.

There were also a lot of photographs spread around, mostly of Willie with various women. A lot of different women.

Willie sat opposite me and seemed to examine my face for signs of rejection or disgust. When he found none, he leaned back and broke the silence. He would like to tell me, he said, a story from his childhood.

"We had real money before the war," he said again, as if it was important for me to know this. "But the fascists came and took it all. It was a very great day for us when we were liberated. My brother and I ran alongside the partisan trucks and yelled at all the handsome communists who rode in them. We wanted them to take us along, but the men just looked grim and serious.

"The spring of '45. There was a lot of commotion and anarchy. No one knew anything. The fascists had melted into the dirt, but the partisans had not yet asserted control. It was an insane time, like Carnival or a revolution.

"I thought it was all marvelous. I was scared, but I was also excited. You could see some incredible things, like fascist women being marched by with shaved heads, and someone had painted the hammer-and-sickle sign on all their foreheads in red ink. I was 12 years old."

He looked at me again, checking to see if I was listening.

"I lost my brother in the crowd. I heard everyone talking about the Piazzale Loreto. 'Loreto, Loreto, Loreto.' This was the cry on everyone's lips.

"Well, I knew where that was, so I went down there. I didn't realize until I arrived, but that's where they had hung the bodies of Mussolini and Claretta. I ran around a corner and suddenly he was right there in front of me. Mussolini, dangling by his bootheels.

"Il Duce! I couldn't believe it! This was where a bombed-out filling station used to be. My family used to buy petrol there. And that was where Il Duce ended up!

"There were a lot of people around, men, women and children, but I squeezed through and looked right up at

Mussolini's face. I had seen that face so often, it was as familiar as my own father's, and now it looked so pathetic.

"A firing squad had executed the two of them, him and Claretta, the night before. The partisans allowed them a night together, him and his fascist whore, in a cottage above Lake Como. It was such an Italian thing to do. Let a man and woman have one last night as a couple before you shoot them!"

Willie laughed briefly. "There were, I don't know, 10 or 12 bodies hanging there alongside of Claretta and Mussolini. I looked up at her. Someone had tied her skirt up with a belt so that it would not flop down and reveal her sex. Some rude country partisan's belt, cinched around this elegant woman's thighs.

"Everyone was yelling and the cathedral bells were going and going. It was quite an exciting time. I remember being overpowered, my body was shaking so hard. The image of those two hanging there burned itself into my mind.

"Then suddenly the crowd just went crazy. Old women began to rush up and spit at Mussolini's face. Some peasant kept trying to get his foot in the air high enough to kick Mussolini's head, and then somebody else decided to help him and drag the body down.

"So they tore Mussolini down, and people started kicking and jabbing and jumping up and down on the body. The whole mob went mad. I was there being shoved and buffeted by all these crazy people, and I watched what they did to that corpse. There wasn't much blood left in the body, so when they would cut him he didn't bleed.

"One old lady took this revolver that looked like it was from the first World War, and she shot Mussolini five times—once for each son she had lost, she said. People were shrieking like lunatics.

"Then, as I was standing there, several women, one right after another, hiked up their skirts and urinated all over Mussolini's face.

"I was transfixed. I had never seen women relieve themselves in public before, of course, but all rules were off here. I saw the urine squirt out and splash all over him. Some partisan took his rifle butt and put it underneath Mussolini's jaw so that the liquid would fall full on his face. I think that was the first time I ever saw a woman's private parts."

"With all the crowd and all the jostling, and all the excitement, I must confess I got an erection and stained my trousers repeatedly with my product."

That's how Willie said it. *Stained my trousers repeatedly with my product.* He was getting a little overheated by the memory, I could tell. The significance of all this was not too difficult to grasp. He was giving an explanation, a sort of résumé of his sexuality. What had made him the way he was.

"What finally ended it was they brought somebody else in, this big government official in the regime, and shot him. He climbed off the truck, gave the fascist salute to Mussolini's mutilated corpse, and then they fired machine gun bullets into him until he died. I saw all this!

"I thought that maybe the crowd would riot even more with the new blood, but somehow, seeing this official get killed seemed to satisfy everyone. Nobody kicked Mussolini anymore. They hung his body back up. I think pretty soon after that the Americans came and took the corpse away.

"I remember an old lady looking up at Claretta's body, hanging in the sky. This mistress of Mussolini, a big powerful lady, well now she was hanging there for everyone to see. She had nice blonde ringlets in her hair, I remember, and her underwear, where it peeked out, was this light, light blue color, like cornflowers.

"This old lady next to me looks up, and she said, 'All that and not even a run in her stockings.'"

Willie laughed as if this were the punchline of a long joke. "It was true," he said, still laughing. "That body was remarkably well preserved."

He stared into his snifter, and the smile he wore faded into a twisted grimace. We remained silent for a while. "That's quite a story," I finally said.

"Isn't it?" he replied, a little too brightly. He set his drink down.

"I wonder if you would please accompany me downstairs?"

I drew back from him. "Oh," I said, trying to keep my tone light, "I wouldn't know what to do."

"I will guide you," Willie said. He sat there with the ice-blue eyes fixed on me. The Look had completely taken over his face now, and he was entreating me.

"Please. I will instruct you what to do."

I didn't know what to say. Besides three martinis and a cognac, I had a lot of conflicting emotions inside of me. One of them, a strong one, was the desire that the Look always gave me, the urge to slap that upturned face in front of me hard, several times.

But there were other impulses telling me to bolt through those heavy double doors and hit a taxi running. I can't quite claim fastidiousness, but there was the idea in my mind that I didn't want to get sullied by this man's bent and tortured psyche. I was better than that, wasn't I? Even if it was a game, it was one that I didn't want to play.

Willie cleared his throat. "I'll make it worth your while," he said, imploring.

I hesitated before going. That was the extent of my innocence.

To Supreme Mistress Sonya,

We really want to be your slaves.

We are a French submissive couple. I, Olivier, am 42, a manager, wealthy and generous.

Marie, my wife, is 35, beautiful, she doesn't work.

We are both submissive and into the Scene for more than ten years.

We are not in heavy but soft S&M, and we would like a mistress to own us.

We go sometimes to N.Y.C., we like this city so much.

We're living in Paris, where we have a big flat; we have a mansion in Normandy, and a boat.

And if you take us in as your slaves, we would be proud to invite you in Paris, anytime you want, all year long.

We expect a long relationship, and we are at your disposal.

On our knees, we kiss the feet of the Goddess.

Olivier & Marie

I was destined for it.

If biology is destiny, then as soon as one particular zooid of my father's sperm won the race to unite with my mother's egg, I was marked to be what I have become... a professional dominatrix, a woman who deals out domination over men.

Domination. Not just pain—pain is sometimes the least part of it. What it is really, is reversal. A kick over the traces of the usual sexual roles, so that the woman becomes victorious, unchallengeable, supreme.

I was destined for it because I grew up tall and blonde and with an imperious cast to my features. Sometimes I think I could have been born in the middle of the rain forest in equatorial Africa and they would have found me, crawled to me, my mewling submissives. Bent, scattered iron filings dragging themselves inexorably toward magnet steel.

They made me. As much as the union of my mother and father, the imploring Look in eyes of these men made me into what I am today. Ever since the amphetamine rush of pubescence, they have been approaching me, across rooms at parties, in smoky lounges, in the street.

It is as if I was born into a secret conclave, and had no choice of membership. Maybe if I had been left alone, maybe if I hadn't been dunned by those imploring eyes at every turn, I could have led an ordinary life. I might have wound up a suburban matron with a bridge afternoon and a garden club day.

When I look back upon the chain of circumstances that led to my becoming a dominatrix, I can point to any number of steps along the way and say that my life seemed to be ruled not by choice but by chance. There were junctures which, if I had hesitated or turned the other way, I might not have ever stumbled upon the murky, extravagant, twilight world of S-M.

But in another sense, it was all fated to happen and it all happened the way it was fated.

S-M. That's the hip way to say it now, you know, among cognoscenti of The Scene. Not "S&M," because you don't say, "sadism and masochism," you say "sado-masochism."

As I look at that hyphenated phrase, "sado-masochism," down on paper now, it seems to have unavoidable connotations. It gives rise to Gothic, nightmarish visions of Nazi doctors—or of whining, quivering jellyfish humans, begging for more torture and pain.

It all seems oddly distant and removed from what I do, five days a week, from the first wave of the "morning rush"—

clients who want sessions before work—to the noon-hour quickies, on through to the after-work specials.

They come marching through my apartment, having first inundated me with 30, 40, sometimes 50 phone calls per day, regulars and first-timers, eager and painfully priapic, one after another, an endless parade of beggars. But I find it difficult to sign them up under the rubric "masochist," just as it seems utterly foreign to classify myself under that weird, prickly and inhuman genus of "sadist."

In fact, it is sometimes difficult to locate myself in the milieu of S-M at all. I am "Mistress Sonya," but even in my own mind the name has inverted commas around it. In some still untouched center of me, I am a Brooklyn girl who reached her majority in the wilds of upstate New York, who returned to the City to pursue a life in art, who somehow got trapped in a web of Downtown decadence, and who found herself trafficking in a strange sort of outlaw sexual transaction.

This is unacceptable. I can have no mundane personal history. I must be the creature of your imaginings. I must be Sonya, She-Wolf of the SS, encased in a carapace of black leather, flashing her blood-encrusted lash, stepping out of some dim Aryan mythology into the sexual pressure cooker of modern American life.

The truth is—happy to say, sad to say—more banal than that, and at the same time much more bizarre. The truth has little in common with the overheated fantasies of those outside the Scene, or the Life, or whatever you want to call it.

Fueled by Phil Donahue and Sally Jessy Raphael, the "truth" as Mr. and Mrs. Front Porch America knows it is lurid, extreme, straight out of Grand Guignol. S-M is a tatty pair of stiletto heels spiking into the pasty flesh of a sicko-pervo-psycho. It's men and women in outlandish garb whacking each other with cat-o-nine-tails. It has something medieval and alien about it.

Above all, it is what other folks do. S-M has no overlap at all with white-bread, vanilla, middle-American culture. In a Venn diagram, the two entities would be discrete and discontinuous.

I'm here to let you down gently. I'm here to say that the people in the Scene might be working next to you, that they might come out of your car pool instead of some Transylvanian castle. At the same time, I want to clue you in that the brand of S-M these people practice might not be all that awful to begin with.

The Scene. That's how people inside refer to it, as in, "I've been in the Scene for 13 years now."

The Scene is a loose affiliation of dominatrices, submissives, clubs, dungeons, boutiques and magazines. Its outposts are scattered all over the country but mainly concentrated in the large cities, with the two primary nodes being San Francisco and New York.

Al Goldstein, the publisher of *Screw*, once wrote about the Scene as "a Beast coiled around the bowels of nighttime America," but I like to think of it as a shadow world, similar to those parallel realities so beloved of science fiction writers.

Lately the shadow has been seeping out into broad daylight. Over the past two decades, the fashions of the Scene have somehow been co-opted by the mainstream, so that you can buy studded leather bracelets at any mall in the country.

Part of this is the natural fascination with the taboo. S-M role-playing is so brutally rejected, so thoroughly discredited by religiously scrupulous or politically correct moralists, that it bubbles below the surface before blowing, volcano-style, right up into everyone's face.

The new visibility of S-M has led to a splitting of the Scene. One half is the heavy metal/biker/teen-rebellion contingent, which puts on S-M as a way of declaring itself separate from vanilla America.

The other half—a little suspicious, a little resentful of the newcomers—is the old-style practitioners, who see S-M not as a choice but a biological necessity. Old-style S-M is an ancient fetish, but it only got codified in a large-scale commercial way since the so-called sexual revolution of the late 60s and 70s.

I straddle both halves of the shadow world. As a sometime member of the Downtown art scene, I used to dabble in the iconography of S-M. I wore the leather pants, the studded collars, the harridan makeup. Even before I was a dominatrix, I sometimes dressed like one, simply because it was the style. Fashion is destiny.

Imagine my surprise when Willie opened that door to his basement playroom and I suddenly got sucked into the other half of the shadow world, the serious, playing-for-keeps, we-do-this-because-we-have-to part of the Scene. It was like a karaoke singer suddenly thrust onto the stage at Carnegie Hall. The shadow world suddenly got darker, stranger, inkier and kinkier.

The reactions of people outside the Scene to me being in it are always a source of amusement to me. I remember having to explain to my lawyer just exactly what it is I do. We were in his office, in one of those lower-Park Avenue attorney ghettos where the directory in the lobby spews out a roll-call of white-shoe names.

"I'm a professional dominatrix," I said.

"I see," he said. He wanted to hear more. Oh, for chrissakes, I thought, look it up in the dictionary.

"It's a form of therapy that deals in pain and submission," I went on, choosing my words carefully.

"Do you need a license from the state for this?" he asked, and I almost laughed in his face. Maybe in some unimaginable future age, I thought, the whole thing would be as simple as going down to City Hall for a marriage license.

"No," I said. "The State of New York doesn't exactly applaud what I do."

He blinked at me. I looked at the Yale Law School diploma on the wall, the embossed lettering of his personalized leather legal folders. You can make a lot of money and still be a fool. Or, like the old joke, if you're so rich, how come you're not smart?

"Men come to me with certain... needs," I said. "And I satisfy them."

"Oh," he said, thoughtfully, seeming or at least pretending to get it. I could see the neon word "hooker" light up in his mind.

"It's not exactly sex," I said. "Not in a form that you or I would recognize it. Some of them want to be spanked."

"Spanked?" he squeaked, beginning to get it now.

"But it's not all whips and chains and pain, either," I said. "It's psychological domination. Whatever it takes. It's different for almost everybody who comes to me, but it's the same in that they are all men who want to be dominated by a woman. They get off on that."

"I see," he said. I watched him slide me into a neat pigeonhole, in a mind that was made up of a whole roost of pigeonholes.

Dear Mistress Sonya:

I am eager to succumb and worship your beauty. I am 39-years-old and live in the New York area. I have been into the Scene for several years, but unfortunately, I have not had the opportunity to meet a Mistress with whom I might develop a lasting relationship. Your power and beauty have totally captivated me, and I am eager to submit myself to your training and servitude.

The slight implication of your pose and posture is exactly the image of beauty that controls and dominates me. I have a strong fetish for high heel shoes, stockings and being tormented and sexually subjugated. To be able to serve at your feet and learn to worship your beautiful body is where I belong.

The need to be physically dominated, erotically seduced, forcibly made to worship and totally controlled are but a few of my desires. There is a physical alertness and responsiveness to you that is inescapable. I need and beg you to seduce and control me in a constant state of arousal through your beauty and power. To be used as a sex toy, as a plaything is a state of being that you know how to properly achieve.

In Eternal Subservience,
Thomas M.

I t is difficult to explain what goes on in a session between me, a dominatrix, and my client, a submissive, because people think they know exactly what happens, and mostly they are wrong.

As soon as they hear what it is I do, they type me. This is true even though they may not be dyed-in-the-wool moralists.

I have a neighbor in New York City, who lives down the hallway from me. He knows what I do and knows that I sometimes work out of my apartment. Meaning I have clients who come in for sessions.

Now a lot of people would have problems with this. They would imagine drooling, bug-eyed johns, leaving a trail of rectified urinal scum back and forth from my apartment door to the elevator, maybe committing a murder-rape or two along the way.

But my friend, whom I'll call Jerry, doesn't mind. He's gay, which right off the bat leaves him more open to what 20th-century America euphemistically calls "alternative lifestyles." He also has a booming career as a photo stylist, and he sometimes also works out of his apartment.

One afternoon he was setting up a photo shoot and needed an angle from our shared fire escape for a lighting set-up. He called to ask if he could send an assistant over and possibly use one of my electrical outlets.

The assistant was a cut-and-buffed Nautilus product who was nevertheless a little damp behind the ears. I watched him walk in with his halogen lamp, see the area of my apartment out of which I work—my office, so to speak—and stop dead in his tracks.

Now, I should explain that I take the minimalist approach when it comes to things like racks, and stocks, and whips and chains. I don't keep a dungeon in my home, and I believe that the whole dungeon atmosphere so well beloved by many Scene habitués is overrated. The real whip is the internal one. The real sting is in the mind.

So I don't go in for elaborate set-ups. What I have in my apartment—what the young p.a. saw—is one stark white wall with a four-by-four of blonde wood bolted into it, and hooks driven into that wood, with various outfits hanging from the hooks.

There is a butterfly rack on a wall at right angles to this. Hanging from the ceiling directly in the center of the area is a galvanized steel chain with a hook at the end of it—a rather evil-looking hook, I'll admit—which is used for suspension practices.

I have worked with this set-up and lived with it for so long—I walk by it every time I go to the bathroom, head for the kitchen to get a cup of tea, or answer the front door—that I no longer even notice it.

The p.a. noticed it, all right. After setting up his light—a little nervously I thought, glancing over his shoulder at me as he worked—he raced back to Jerry's apartment and said breathlessly, "You should see what she has over there!"

The clients on the photo shoot were two executives from Bloomingdale's, and they did indeed want to see what I had over there, so the whole bunch of them trooped back over to my apartment, Jerry at the lead, to ooh and ahh over my little corner of S-M purgatory, ask me all sorts of questions, and eventually determine that they would like to do a shoot there.

There was not a whiff of condemnation in their reaction to my "alternative" lifestyle, but in a sense I found their over-heated embrace of it just as wrong-headed as finger-pointing from the pulpit. No one gets it right, not the moralists, and not the ones who want to prove how far beyond mere moralism they really are.

In between are the innocents, like my lawyer. I took a casual date up to my apartment once, a stock broker from Great Neck, a well-scrubbed boy who in retrospect I wonder what the hell I was doing with. He took one look at my S-M accouterments and uttered an immortal line (I've in fact forgotten exactly what the boy looks like, whether he was dark or fair, but I remember the line).

"My God," he exclaimed, "you must be very secure in your sexuality!"

What amazes me is the power of a label. I was at a party once, a very proper Park Avenue bash, thrown by a friend of a friend in honor of an artist. As sometimes happens at these kinds of soirees, the Downtown crowd was mixed in with the Upper East Side matrons in a kind of uneasy suspension.

You could immediately identify the Downtown people, little clots of black floating in a sea of chintz. I was definitely one of them, dressed as I was in casual flourishes of leather, silver studs and black silk.

Light-years ago, culturally speaking, such an outfit would have announced me as a member of the Scene straight off. As it was, S-M couture had infiltrated the straight world to the degree that not only was I blandly welcomed by the hostess, in her requisite red Adolfo, but I was also outdressed, leather-and-silver-stud-wise, by her just-in-from-prep-school daughter.

Left to drift by my escort, I found myself in conversation with a totally bald, stooped, doddering physician emeritus of 60 or so, bowtied, with the flushed face and the pink pate that signaled a myocardial infarction-in-the-making.

"I'm a naughty boy," he announced as his opening conversational gambit, and for a moment I thought he might be an ex-client of mine, using his sexual tag-line in an effort to reestablish recognition.

But no, he was only referring to the dripping piece of foie-gras he was cramming into his mouth. In this case, it didn't resemble a mouth, but what my father used to call a "pie-hole." It reminded me of the mouth that Jon Voight crammed a telephone receiver into in *Midnight Cowboy*.

"Not supposed to eat this, but I can't resist," Pie-Hole mumphed, sucking down the liver noisily. "Very naughty of me."

Usually, I try to keep my professional life apart from my private one. I don't know why, but this time I rose to the bait. "Maybe you ought to be spanked," I said lightly.

I could actually see his body surge with delight. His stoop straightened perceptibly; I think he might have become an inch or two taller. The sort of senile nutation that old men sometimes suffer made his head appear to wag playfully.

"I should," he crowed, "I should be spanked!"

"Bend over my knee right here," I said, "In front of all these people."

Another paroxysm passed through his body. Better back off, I told myself, if you don't want a dead doctor on your hands.

But he seemed greedy for it, and we embarked on a merry five-minute tour of his musty, dusty, creaky old sexual psyche. I thought of the bad-luck octogenarian in the joke—the one time he gets an erection, his hand has fallen asleep. In this particular improvised skit, I was the domineering mother-figure, and Dr. Pie-Hole was the naughty little boy. Pretty soon the old guy's adult diaper was going to need changing.

Then my date, Andrew, glided up out of nowhere. "You've met Irving," he said. (As in most places in this book, the names here are altered. It's a true story, to paraphrase Jack Webb, only the names have been changed to protect the impotent.)

Looking at Irving and me, Andrew said, "I thought you two would get along."

Was that a leer I saw in Andrew's face? Did he know something I didn't? Dr. Irving, meanwhile, was visibly disappointed that our play of cloud and rain had ended.

"You know what Sonya does for a living, don't you?" Andrew asked. "It's pretty kinky, Doc, I don't know if you're ready for it."

"Nothing human is foreign to me," Irving said loftily, quoting what I later found out was a line from the Roman poet Terence, the world's first black literati. Dr. Pie-Hole had left his little-boy mode behind, and activated his genial physician's arrogance.

"She's a dominatrix," Andrew said, grinning. "She takes old men like you and whips them into shape."

I will always remember the change that Dr. Irving underwent then. He reared back with a frostiness that totally denied what had previously passed between us.

"Interesting," he said in a clipped way, which indicated that it was not, indeed, interesting at all, it was appalling. Then he turned heel and ran. I was philosophical about it, and finished my champagne alone, staring out the windows onto the glittering string of ruby brake lights on the avenue below.

The good doctor was not going to leave it there, however. I saw him sidle up to the hostess and speak to her urgently. The hostess passed her eyes in my direction. When Andrew and I left soon afterwards, he was surprised to be told by her highness not to bring me around again.

I was rather startled by this breach of noblesse oblige, but it fit in with what I had experienced about the straight world's arm's-length appreciation of S-M. The doc was fine when he was playing out his private fantasies with a woman he met at a party. When Andrew put a label on me—"dominatrix, the demon she-bitch from hell"—things changed.

Dear Sonya;

    You will I hope pardon my bluntness; it comes from need...intense need. I have seen a photograph of you, and I cannot help myself—I would like to see you, to kneel at your feet, to drink you. To love you as only one who submits can.
    Will you help me?
    I look forward to hearing from you, and will I hope have the honor to remain...

Very truly yours,
Marcus S.

here's a club in downtown Manhattan that bills itself as "the friendly S-M Club." I wouldn't put a moronic happy face on an intense, deeply seated sexual fetish, but I would like to remove the death mask in which S-M is seen skulking around the tabloids.

The face of this fetish, like all fetishes, is a human one, and the sooner we recognize that, the sooner we can lift the fog of guilt from a lot of people's lives.

Extirpating guilt might not be at the top of your list of goals for the week, and a lot of times it seems that society as a whole—especially the neo-Puritanical society of America in the Age of AIDS—is constructed as a vast engine for the creation of guilt.

I used to have a friend who, after midnight discussions over the sad state of the world and the sadder state of humanity, used to fall silent and after a long moment sigh, "Oh, those humans."

Oh, those humans seem to have a peculiar insistence on maintaining the status of the Other at all cost. We must have scapegoats, we must have outcasts, we must have enemies. Sometimes it seems that human life is an elaborate charade perpetrated for the purpose of separating the sheep from the goats, the white hats from the black, the self from the Other.

I have seen this impulse act time and time again upon straight people's approach to S-M. They don't want to see it as part of their world at all. They relish its alien mystery, its separation from themselves.

To admit that the sexual dynamic of S-M influences their lives would be just too terrifying. Not only would it challenge the safe and secure foundation of their safe and secure world, it would deprive them of that Otherness, that ability to point a finger, which serves to keep their own world stable.

But it's not us against them, it's only us, as Bill Clinton (whose wife, Hillary, was once pictured on the cover of *Spy* magazine in full S-M regalia) said.

Andrew told me later that Dr. Pie-Hole was an extremely successful, extremely competitive radiologist who headed up the department in a prestigious local hospital.

"A real hard-ass guy on the job," Andrew reported. "Treats his help like dirt, then comes home and is sweetness and light to his family."

"A pillar of the community," I said. I could imagine him verbally lashing some young nurse in his employ, or relishing an internecine battle for control of the department. The mutability of the roles of dominance and submission struck me anew.

Oh, those humans.

Many of the men I saw, who came to me as submissives, were absolute martinets at work. They were dictators, candidates for the world's most horrible boss. Dr. Irving the physician-powerhouse or Dr. Irving the "naughty little boy." Two sides of the same coin. Or the same con.

I could have refused Dr. Irving's conversational gambit, not taken up the glove he threw down. There's an old joke: What does a sadist do to the masochist? Nothing. Because the masochist derives pleasure from pain. So therefore the greatest pain a sadist can give is to refuse to be a partner in the dance.

For a long time, that's what I did. All my life, that long parade of males has filed past me. I've resigned myself to the fact that certain men will always approach me with a yearning, with some unsatisfied desire they think I can fill.

At first I was baffled by this seemingly endless succession of need that marched up to my door. Then I was bored with it, then angered by it. Biology is destiny, and some quirk of biology has made me the spitting image of some men's dreams. And a lot of those men want Brunhild to play Valkyrie on their backsides.

I don't want to play victim here, and absolve myself of all responsibility. Clearly, I made a choice to enter into the complicated transactions of commercial S-M. But I do want to enter one woman's sense of wonder at the terrible persistence of men's need.

Are dominatrices born, or made? How about both? I was destined for it, but I had help along the way, too. The constant dunning of the human male made me into what I am today. The endless waves of yearning eroded whatever sense of self I had, until I found myself able to kick off my heels with Dr. Irving and accomplish what amounted to a psycho-sexual minuet.

What does a sadist do to a masochist? Nothing. But sometimes it's just too hard to resist.

Dearest Goddess Sonya,

i am a 31 year old white male. i am 6'1" tall and weigh about 205 pounds. i work out regularly and am in good physical shape.

i have been into Female domination for over 13 years now.

My first actual experience was 12 years ago at The Chateau in San Francisco. i was there on business and took the opportunity to live out my fantasy. i have been addicted to Female Domination ever since!

More recently, i have been serving Mistress R_____ V_____ in Connecticut. She is going to be moving to Florida in the near future. So once again i am looking for an attractive, skillful Dominant Goddess to serve.

i was extremely excited to find you! Not only are you a very beautiful Dominant Goddess but you specialize in my favorite activity, creative S&M!

i very much hope that you will consider allowing me the privilege of serving as your slave!

i am into pretty much anything to do with Female Domination. i am always interested in being subjected to new experiences and having my limits expanded to please my Goddess!

Some of my favorite activities include, but are by

no means limited to: *Female Body Worship, Bondage, Flagellation, Cock & Ball Bondage/Torture/Teasing.*

Thank you very much for taking the time to read my letter!

i very much hope that your will consider allowing me the opportunity to serve as your slave!

Very Sincerely,
slave robert

T he session with Willie—
my first-ever experience as a dominatrix—was short and surreal.

"I want you to do this to me," he would say, and then he would direct me in curt, hurried sentences, as if his having to tell me somehow violated the quality of his subservience.

Even through the haze of alcohol I knew there were boundaries which I would not cross. I left the whole wall of implements largely alone, and would have nothing to do with enemas or anything that involved body liquids.

I tied him up. I didn't have a big history with the Girl Scouts, and had no brother in the Boy Scouts, either, so my knot-tying abilities were rudimentary in the extreme. I wasn't, as they say, prepared.

It didn't matter. When I lashed Willie to the rack he was there to stay. At one point I fumbled with a knot and he suggested some heavy-duty handcuffs which were hanging on the wall. I told him to shut up, and his body performed a little spasm-dance of pleasure.

The strange thing was that I found a large part of it, the important part of it, totally natural. Not the whips and the chains and the wooden stocks—that part was foreign to me then and to some extent still is, even though I deal with it everyday—but the psychological dynamics.

The imploring, begging, wheedling Look had completely taken over Willie's eyes. My answer to it came naturally. I wanted to hurt him. And this impulse of mine, direct, immediate, funneled straight up from my subconscious, was what Willie was looking for. It's what makes me a good dominatrix. It's what they pay me for.

To react to vulnerability with anger. To lash out at the weak. To slap the upturned face, to curse the supplicant, to victimize the victim.

You may deny it as a part of yourself, but I have seen it too many times, in too many areas of social interaction and human endeavor, not to conclude that it is a basic part of us all. It may be modified by some sort of behavioral intervention—in fact, this may be what civilization is all about—but even though it is blocked or channeled, it is always there.

Willie looked a little Jesus-like when I tied him, spread-eagled, on his rack. Every accouterment he possessed was so elaborate. I remember admiring the rack's smoothly finished oak surface, which implied solidity, permanence, tradition. It was the opposite of the ticky-tacky with which most things in America were built. A Continental torture rack.

It was odd, standing there in a man's S-M playroom and admiring his taste in decorating (the place could've been featured in *Better Homes and Dungeons*), but I was in an odd mood. A large part of it, as I recall, was risible. I was laughing to myself as I tied him up, as I took the whip when he directed me and applied it to his backside.

This is bizarre, this is all so mind-bogglingly odd, I would laugh to myself. Or, quoting the Dead, *What a long strange trip it's been.* Chortling inside all the while.

If I hadn't been a little drunk, I think I would have found it appalling. Not in any moral sense (because I find that whole bourgeois morality dodge tiresome and boring), but in a practical sense.

Willie's situation offended my sense of proportion. What a waste, I thought, that this guy has all this opportunity, that almost anything in the world is within his reach, and this is what it takes to get him off.

The hair on his testicles was silver, and suddenly the sight of that struck me as impossibly ugly. I became revulsed. At that point, Willie the misguided theatrical director was instructing me in the fine art of nipple torture, and I just broke. I tore savagely at his flesh with my fine white teeth.

"Mistress," he mewled, "Oh, Mistress."

Afterwards, in the Matisse room, Willie smoked a cigar, and I felt like I had earned one, too. He disappeared and came back with a heavy cream-colored envelope stuffed with $100 bills. Crisp, new, cash-machine bills, ten of them. I did not hesitate in accepting them. My innocence, I guess, did not extend that far.

During the whole time we spent in his chamber, Willie had not touched me. I would have liked to report that the experience did not touch me sexually, either, but that was not the case. I remember thinking after Willie climaxed that I would have liked to come, too. But there was no allowance made for that. Willie had no interest whatsoever in satisfying me.

It was my first experience with the inherent selfishness of the sexual submissive. It would not be my last. I have come to know the attitude well, to the point where I am led to the only conclusion possible, that submissiveness is really the ultimate guise of power.

In all my sessions with everyone I have ever seen professionally, I have noticed it. The last shall come first. Here I was, supposedly the dominatrix, but I was locked into Willie's version of the sex act. One may smile and smile and be a villain, says Shakespeare. One may grovel and grovel and be the boss, says Sonya.

Willie neglected to get me a cab when he pecked me good-bye at the door of his townhouse. He looked rosy-cheeked and smugly satisfied. The Look had withdrawn from his eyes like a bear to hibernation, replaced by the ironic, detached Europeaness to which I had first been attracted.

I would have liked to spend more time with this post-coital Willie, this suave, witty, self-contained gent of means, but it was not to be. He assured me he would call, and I knew he would—as soon as the bear awoke and his need required.

But he would never call me just for a fun night on the town. A gust of loneliness blew down the rain-damp street and passed right through me. The loneliness of the whore. It was the first time I experienced that, too.

I said good-bye and he closed the door before I was down the steps. There were plenty of cabs now that the rain had stopped and the late-night crowd had thinned. I caught one at Park that was going the wrong way, uptown.

Once I got inside, I barked out directions at the driver to make a U-turn, in a voice that surprised me with its forcefulness. The poor guy executed the maneuver with the alacrity of a henpecked husband, and we headed back downtown.

There were plenty of things to think about on the 30-block ride to my apartment. There was the heavy cream-colored envelope, full of rich-man's cash. There was the fact that I had not been touched, mussed, or messed with. I had been in control. There was the fact that the transaction had been simple. At a level that rather disturbed and astonished me, what Willie and I had performed together had been among the most honest sexual transactions of my life.

The money in the envelope would pay a good chunk of my rent for that month. I wondered how many more envelopes like it there were scattered around the streets of Manhattan.

And why stop there? What about the streets of Paris, Madrid, London, Rio, the world? I forgot the loneliness of earlier in the night and concluded that the evening had been relatively painless to me.

Disgust and revulsion were momentary feelings that would pass. Loneliness, even if I bothered to recall it, was part of the human condition. I felt a surge of excitement at life's possibilities. *This would not be the end of it,* I thought.

The phrase from the Dead floated up again. The cab dove into the black hole of the Helmsley Building tunnel and ran up along the roadway around Grand Central. What a long strange bizarre surreal silly trippy trip it's been.

When people do that, when they quote that Robert Hunter line, I usually react with an inner sneer. It always seems so myopic and self-aggrandizing to me.

Well, pal, I feel the urge to say, don't flatter yourself. It hasn't been *that* strange of a trip. I mean, your little jaunt still fits well within the bounds of human experience. You haven't been tele-transported to the rings of Saturn or anything, have you?

So, okay, I was being dramatic. The trip that led me to Willie's doorstep and, afterwards, into the life of a professional dominatrix, wasn't all that strange. In fact, in a lot of ways, it has been crushingly, screamingly mundane. Instead of the Dead, try Lou Reed: *There was nothing going down at all, not at all.* Her life was saved by rock 'n' roll. How ordinary.

But by other lights, each of us is a precious snowflake, so unlike the everyone else, unique unto ourselves. As you learn in kindergarten.

When I look back on it, even the not-that-strange quality of my upbringing seems bizarre to me, given what I've become. If normal, average, grade-school-attending girls can grow up to become dominatrices, what does that say about normalcy?

Please remember to speak in a very soft voice before, during and after our session.

Pretend we work in the same office. I've been molesting you at work and you want to put a stop to it. I've invited you over to my place, thinking we'll go to bed. I start touching you. You tell me that you are dating the president of our company. I call you a whore and you slap me (hard) across the face. You tell that you have just been promoted and that now you are my boss. You start slapping me around (12 to 15 heavy slaps, a few backhands, too). When I'm good and beat, you force me to worship you (boot licking, hand kissing, a little taste of breast, mouth and pussy, too). Then, with you sitting on the bed or couch and me sitting on the floor, kick me (gently) in the face 12-15 times. Make the last one a hard one, hard enough to knock me over. Then, kick me around the room. I'll roll around the floor in the direction of the bathroom. When we there, kick me into the tub and stuff the wash cloth into my mouth.

Then, while I'm masturbating, humiliate me by breaking two dozen eggs over my head (eggs are in refrigerator).

I was the product of a union between a jock and a showgirl, the type of match-up that is, if I read my *People* magazine correctly, still going strong—only now they call themselves athletes and models. And the product of a Brooklyn childhood, which is also still going strong, and I don't need *People* to tell me that.

Joan, my mother, was a high-WASP femme fatale with a runway model's figure and extremely well-sculpted cheekbones. Two-hundred dollars-a-week cheekbones, and legs to match. She was for much of her active career a Billy Rose showgirl.

When I let this fact slip recently in casual conversation, the gent I told it to immediately responded, "You know, Billy Rose fucked all his girls."

Thanks ever so for the inside information. Extremely gracious of you, but I don't really need to know the gynecological facts behind my mommy's career, thank you very much. Like about 100 percent of the human race, I'm squeamish when it comes to the whole idea of my mother fucking anyone but my father, and even there, it's not something I exactly like to dwell on.

I knew my mother as a woman about town, a chorine, as they used to call them. She spent a long while as a model in the Garment District after her showgirl career. Joan modeled for Norman Norell and Charles James. She was a person eminently comfortable in all-male milieus. In the world of the 50s, when I was growing up, a woman trying to make her way in the world was like a staked goat. She was open prey to any wolf who happened by.

When I try to imagine the Garmentos of back then—not that they've changed much today—I can picture Joanie making her way among them, fighting them off, scratching out a living for herself and her family.

She was out there because my father was a failed athlete. He took a little while getting over the fact that the world of sports was not going to be a life-long meal ticket for him.

Frederick was a German-born émigré who, along with his brother Alec, was billed as one of the "Shellogg Twins." They weren't really twins, but they were effective linemen at Notre Dame. And even though Alec played with the Chicago Bears, and Fred with the Giants, they never quite made it in the big leagues.

Oh, my father did indeed get a contract with the New York Giants for two seasons after college, but that was just the tease before the door slammed in his face. I still have the contract, a faded yellow document signed by Wellington Mara, which indicates that the team paid my father $500 for a full season of play. Fred was on the same team as Mel Hein and Tuffy Leemans. But a bad knee closed him out of the only life he had ever known.

The disappointment rendered Daddy useless for quite a while. He would sit around our apartment in Turner Towers—the residence of Howard Cosell and 17 floors of the most ferocious Jews imaginable—on Eastern Parkway, right off Grand Army Plaza in Brooklyn.

Fred would occasionally run vague errands for people. When I later thought about it as an adult I concluded he was a bagman, but my mother dismissed this idea as ridiculous.

"Your father was just a big mug," she said, which reads a little more kindly than how it came off when she said it.

Being a child with a clear view of the matter, I liked my father a lot, especially his whole approach to parenting, which could be summed up with the phrase, "Don't tell your mother about this."

Of course, I didn't know he was a bum at the time. I didn't know that his not working meant Mommy had to go out and get pawed by random Garmentos and Billy Rose and whomever else she couldn't fight off.

Even if I did make the connection, I would have brought up the fact (if I had known it back then) that my mother was no shrinking violet herself, that she got around quite a bit before she married my father. She later told me that during her heyday she had dated Walter Winchell, John Garfield and Joseph Cotton.

What I also didn't know until later was that I was born with a broken collarbone, because my mother was on the runway working as a model right up until she was five months pregnant with me. The tight-fitting girdle she wore to keep me from showing to the world crushed me in utero.

Daddy would sit around the Turner Towers apartment all day long. He would read the newspaper cover to cover, even the ads, like Ibsen. Unlike Ibsen, he did not produce any world-class theater. All Daddy liked to produce were ace-high flushes. Every day from about 3 to 6, he'd get a medium-stakes poker game going.

These games were important to me, because they were where I began to bond with men. I have always gotten along much better with men than I have with women. Whenever I smell cigar smoke or a pipe, I flash back to that warm paternal world when Daddy took care of me, a full house beat a flush and Mommy was out at rehearsal.

I never realized as a child how huge my father was. To me, he was just my father, and I didn't have any real perspective. but whenever anyone came to my house, they would say, "Who's that man?"

They'd be really staggered by the sheer size of him. I'd say, "That's my father," like it was no big deal, but I think being intimate with male physical power and prowess at that young

age inured me to it somehow, so I was never intimidated or
even that impressed by it in later life.

Whatever my mother thought of my father—and there
was plenty of her testimony on the matter, rendered at the top
of her lungs—I knew it couldn't be all that simple, that he
was a bum and thus the source of all our misfortune. I knew
he must have something on some other kind of ball than a
football.

For example, he had the foresight to leave Germany in
1936, when he was still a teenager. He also had the inventive-
ness to secure a berth on a ship to America, and once there,
hop a freight to South Bend and be "discovered" as a football
prospect.

Later, in the war years, he kept his Teutonic background
quiet, and didn't mention the fact that he had entered the
1936 Olympics on the German team. He managed to get
himself accepted in the Army Air Corps, and spent World
War II serving in Biloxi, Mississippi.

Eastern Parkway when I was growing up was a haven of
upper-class Jewishness that allowed me an idyllic childhood,
stimulating, exciting, expansive. We were one of four Gentile
families in the building. I know, because my little sister Kathy
and I took a census of the names on the lobby register. I was
the oldest of four children, but the other two came along
much later. For a while it was just Kathy and me, the Brooklyn
Museum, the Prospect Park Zoo and the Botanical Gardens.

Apart from my parent's rock-sock-'ems (which never
really seemed that serious, since the two of them always made

up afterwards), the only cloud that floated in my childhood sky was an incident when I came near to being raped in 1959. There had been other rapes of little girls in Brooklyn—the innocence of the 1950s was ending, making way for the Brave New World to come—and the man who had committed them was probably the same one who molested me in the lobby of Turner Towers one warm sunny day.

What saved me was my thick white Carter underpants, double-weight cotton jobbies that we all wore back then. They were the equivalent of natural-fabric chastity belts.

I remember the smell of the brilliantine on the man's slicked-back hair, his owlish eyes behind black horn-rims, his long bony fingers digging into my crotch, trying to find a way past the Carter armor.

He had me clutched tight, and for some reason I couldn't summon the strength to struggle or shout or fight. My eyes fixed on the brass nameplates on the first floor doors like I was in a daze.

And I remember Ruth Futterman, too, a neighbor who acted as my savior. She walked into the dark of the lobby and said, "Susie?" in a quavering, uncertain voice.

"Don't answer," Brilliantine hissed, but he dropped me and ran.

Ruth found me babbling and crying in the hallway. The police came, and for a single Sunday afternoon I was the talk of the Towers.

Joan went berserk, and blamed my father for not keeping an eye on me. I remember the incident less than I remember traipsing down to the police station every month for a full year with Joan, looking through mug shots and examining new suspects, trying to ID the man who attacked me. After a little while, I began to wonder who it was all for, Joan or me. She was on a crusade of vengeance. I wanted to get on with my life.

Which I did, although not in the way I had envisioned. At age 10, I was dragged kicking and screaming out of my beloved Brooklyn and moved to upstate New York, to a farming hamlet near Albany with the unfortunate name of Coxsackie—pronounced like it's spelled, and located just east of Climax and Surprise.

My father had finally shaken off his lethargy to get a master's degree in education, and then secured a job as a minor bureaucrat in state government. Joan, exhausted after over 12 years of pulling the family load, dropped her Mother Courage act in favor of the role of a small town housewife.

Coxsackie. Just the name can send a stab of revulsion through my guts. It was a small town of 1,600 back then. Today it has grown somewhat as a bedroom community to Albany. A place of wide lawns and narrow minds, as Hemingway used to say about his birthplace. It struck me even at age 10 how proud these people were of their ignorance.

As a fast-mouthed Brooklyn girl, I was thoroughly despised by all the baa-baas I went to school with. Because I was reading at an accelerated level, I was skipped ahead a grade, and this added to their resentment. I was ostracized and mimicked mercilessly. In a way, I should be thankful, because the treatment made me into a bookworm, a quiet, serious child.

I became an imaginary Jew. My Turner Towers upbringing had so immersed me in Jewish culture that I was ashamed of being a Gentile. I hated the practice of having a Christmas tree and I hated the fact that I had to go to school on Jewish holidays.

To me, Jewishness represented everything sophisticated, elegant and cultured. Gentiles were rude and stupid and non-artistic.

At school, I was surrounded by farm girls with large breasts. These girls had no problem mixing dairy with meat; at age 11 or 12, many of them were already on their way to being D-cups. I was an outsider from the city who had no chest to speak of at all.

During gym class one cold spring day, a gang of them got together and physically pushed me out of the window nude. The boys outside complained that there was nothing there for them to see.

Estrogen saved me. When my pubescence burst across my body like a public works project, I began to get a little more popular with the boys, and that lessened the hostility of the girls. Sex thus seemed to me to be a very positive development in my life, and I was in a hurry to capitalize on it.

I gave up my virginity in a quest for the ability to wear Tampax. This was a factor that overshadowed all other considerations—that I would be through with the bulky business of pads forever.

He was the "older guy" straight out of Central Casting, and our tryst was depressingly routine, too. I lost my virginity at age 15 in a car at a Saturday night drive-in movie—and no,

I don't remember what was showing at the time. The only novelty I can claim is that we did not repair to the back seat to do the deed, but stayed in the front, so he could see the screen.

"If I jerk off first into a sock," Thomas assured me, "then you won't get pregnant." I was agreeable. I allowed him the freedom of my newly budded breasts while he worked his dink furiously with his other hand. He pushed the white lace of my bra up around my neck, and then ejaculated into a sock that had been oh-so-conveniently stashed (what's *this* doing here?) in the glove box.

Then I stared off into space, or at the radio dial, while he stabbed at me with his penis. I bled from the wound all over his new seatcovers.

He seemed immediately more concerned with the stain than with my physical or emotional well-being. He had to take his family to church the next morning, he explained, and was worried that the blood might not come out.

I hadn't realized that the switch from Kotex to Tampax would give me away to Joan.

"You know, you're wasting it on these people," she said to me, after the first round of screaming, panicked, shoe-flinging recrimination was over. "You want to be a slut? You can either be a high-class slut or a low-class one—the choice is yours."

Is that my only choice, Mommy? What if I don't want to be a slut at all? Maybe I was my mother's daughter after all, because at the time I didn't even think to ask her that question.

By the time the cab ride home from Willie's had ended, I decided to seize the gold ring which fate held out for me. I would become a professional dominatrix.

Instead of fighting against the dictates of destiny, biology, other people's expectations, etc. why not give in?

So, great. Where do I go from there?

"Do you need a license for that?" my lawyer had wanted to know.

Well, no. But what exactly do you need?

I was clueless. There isn't exactly a number you can call for advice on this sort of thing. Hello, Small Business Administration? Could I have your Office of Sadism Support, please? I need to send away for your Dominatrix Starter Kit.

The journey of a thousand miles doesn't begin with a single step, it begins with a lot of wild staggering around in the dark while you try to figure out how to take the first step.

I gained my footing when I made the simple but momentous decision to treat the whole thing as if I were starting up any other sort of business. Who cares if I was dealing in the merchandising of pain for pleasure? The rules of entrepreneurship, I reasoned, ought to be the same if I were selling Vegematics or encyclopedias.

How do you start a business? Figure out what you are selling, then figure out who your customers are, and bring A and B together. Voilà. Cash flow.

At least in general outline, I knew what I was selling. I might be a little vague on the specifics, but I figured I was pretty good at bullshitting my way through situations.

As George Burns said, "You gotta be sincere. If you can fake that, you've got it made." Puff, puff. I could fake that.

Customers. Well, yes. I had a fool-proof method for getting those, too. Just go through my usual routine, and look into men's eyes until the Look pops up, like a duck in a shooting gallery. Collar the poor schmuck, drag him back to my apartment, slap him upside the head a few times, Hoover out his wallet, and send him on his way.

(As anyone who has ever been in the Working Life can tell you, this is all wrong. Hoover out the wallet first, girlfriend, *then* provide your service. Otherwise you run up against a certain post-coital disinclination to settle up for the fun you've just provided. But this just goes to show you how naive I was when I first started.)

I could have done that, of course. I could have trucked through my normal day-to-day, and waited until fate blocked my path with submissive men. Then, I don't know, maybe have attractive business cards to give out at those opportunities. Something in a bold, cursive script. Assertive, but with a hint of the feminine.

Somehow relying on fate to pander clients struck me as a shade too passive. If I was going to do this thing (was I really going to do this thing?) I ought to jump in with both feet, seven-inch stiletto heels and all. So I needed a more proactive method of gaining customers.

I imagined that there were certain magazines which specialized in such things, but the thought of searching them out depressed me. I could see myself standing on the threshold of one of those seedy storefronts in Times Square, the stench of bleach emanating from inside, while the raincoat brigade jostled each other over the latest issue of *Enema Journal*.

No thanks. I briefly considered the Yellow Pages. I had always thought it hilarious and the true height of American hypocrisy that Ma Bell acts as the biggest pimp in the country.

You don't think so? Let your fingers do the walking to the "E's" in your local phone book. You'll find "Escorts," a very healthy listing, one of the longest in the book. If it's out there, it's in-and-out here.

But the Yellow Pages were screamingly expensive, too much for a lone entrepreneur trying to break into the biz. Not all of us can be the General Motors of the escort game. Besides, I was offering a specific service, one not really covered by the cloying, prick-teasing ads of Ma Bell. I knew there had to be other options.

I had never read the small print in the back of magazines, but I did so now. *The Village Voice*, I realized, had a whole section of call girl, massage parlor, phone sex and "role play" ads in the back of the book.

I usually read the *Voice* the way the rest of New York does—taking out the movie listing and trashing the rest of it. Now, perusing the "adult" ads, I wondered what the politically correct element on the staff thought about their salaries coming from the sweat off their sisters' backs.

But I was on the right track. Euphemisms like "escorts" and "role-playing" allowed the publishers of these rags to have it both ways. They desperately wanted the ad revenue, but wished to place as much distance as possible between themselves and the world of commercial sex.

So publications like the Yellow Pages, the *Village Voice* and *New York* magazine invented a code by which they could maintain their virtue and their profit margins at the same time.

I didn't know this back then. In my innocence, I first tried to place an ad of my own composition in *New York* magazine.

Besides quoting a price that took my breath away (save hard, Sonya, save very hard), the pinched voice of the advertising rep read out a long list of forbidden words. "Domination." "Dominatrix." "Submissive." "Slave." "S-M" itself, with or without the ampersand. I didn't have the heart to ask if "flailing cat-o'-nine-tails" or "cold-steel enema nozzle" were out also.

I learned that for my purposes, "Role Playing" was the signifier for S-M. I pity the poor soul who is not in on the whole ruse. Desperately seeking a dominatrix, he cruises right past the role-playing ads because he isn't in the market for acting classes right at the moment, thank you very much.

But role playing it was, and if they were too dense to figure out the code, I didn't want them drooling on my carpet anyway. I selected *New York* magazine as a fairly neutral venue.

It was also the publication most likely to provide upscale customers who could afford the steep rate I was charging. At least, I looked forward to it being steep, not yet having figured out what exactly I would charge. Get them by the balls, to paraphrase Lyndon Johnson, and the money will follow of its own accord.

CREATIVE ROLE PLAY. ELEGANT AND EXCLUSIVE.

My first six-word attempt. Very simple, unadorned. Screamingly devoid of any meaning at all, in fact, or anything that might offend the delicate sensibilities of *New York* magazine. Or the Catholic League of Decency, for that matter.

"Creative" because, what the hell, in another life I went to art school. "Role play" to indicate S-M. "Elegant" and "exclusive" were also code words, meaning "expensive."

I liked it, and besides, the cheapest two-line ad you could purchase (for $250 per week) had to be eight words tops, with the phone number included as one word. I had a total of seven, and I did feel there was something missing...

An ad exec I once knew told me there was one word you should always try to squeeze into an advertisement, because it got 'em every time. The magic word was "free." Well, I couldn't use that, because I wasn't fucking Florence Nightingale. But he also told me of his second-choice word.

CREATIVE ROLE PLAY. ELEGANT, EXCLUSIVE AND NEW.

"New," according to Mister Madison Avenue, had certain incantatory properties, and thus should be worked into whatever ad you were circulating whenever possible.

So there it was. I had "A"—the thing I was selling—and this ad was going to get me "B," the customers who wanted to buy it.

I went down to the *New York* magazine offices (which turned out to be only blocks away from my apartment, on Second Avenue) and placed the ad, scraping together the money by using part of next month's rent. Willie's munificent stipend was long gone.

But nothing ventured, nothing gained. I figured if I put the message in the bottle and nary a reply floated back in return, then I was only out the chunk of change. Sadder, wiser, poorer, and checking out openings in the typing pool.

New York reaches the newsstands on Monday. I spent a long weekend chewing my nails down to the quick and watching, fascinated, as my telephone assumed larger and larger proportions in my life.

Would it ring? Would it not ring? Which did I really want it to do? My phone mutated and transformed, growing until it almost ate up the apartment, finally settling into a face with a manic, troll-like expression, as if the demon of Willie himself had possessed it.

I waited. Slowly, about 9 p.m. on Sunday night or so, a wave of panic swelled offshore, built itself into tidal proportions and then crashed down on me. I realized that I did not, indeed, have "A" together at all. In fact, I had no idea what I was selling. I didn't have a dungeon, I didn't have a rack. I didn't even have a whip. What's a dominatrix without a lash? Just a screaming bitch.

No listing in the Yellow Pages for "Domination Equipment." I cut a pretty pathetic figure, digging through my closets for riding boots, high heels, *anything*. It was like a parody of performance panic. Briefly, I considered calling Willie up and asking him if I could use his playroom in exchange for a cut of the profits. If there were profits. What the hell was I doing? Mommy!

I took two Halcions, the sleeping pill of presidents and impulse killers (same difference?), and crashed out. My last thought before slipping under was that I ought to make an excellent dominatrix, because I was beating myself up just fine.

I was awakened by the phone.

Any woman who has ever looked full into the face of male sexual need comes away changed. Most of us are familiar with its vague outline, and almost all of us see the occasional specific tentacle grope out of the darkness and attempt to encircle its prey.

But to see the full beast is to court madness.

February 1, 1993

Dear Sonya:

As you recall, I have a fetish for diapers. When we do the fantasy, I would like you to instruct me to disrobe, whereupon you see that I am wearing an adult-sized disposable diaper. You comment on it, and check me to see if I am wet, which I am. You then proceed to change me.

I would like you to describe in detail how you are changing me. In addition to getting my diaper changed, you could also incorporate some light dominance into the fantasy, in the form of a spanking and ordering me to do some light housework. I would also appreciate it if you could again give me another diaper change.

By all means be spontaneous and creative. I will be calling you in the days ahead, and I look forward to doing the session with you.

Sincerely,
Brian M.

From the moment *New York* magazine hit the streets, my phone did not stop ringing. It rang at all hours, odd hours, even hours. Sometimes it would startle me by ringing as soon as I set it down into its cradle.

My friends complained that they could no longer reach me because my phone was always busy. I began to realize one of the requisites of the business was having a dedicated phone line.

That first morning, climbing out of my Halcion daze like Norman Bates climbing out of a dress, I stared at the jangling telephone terror as if it were the evidence of some crime. I couldn't face talking to anyone. Let it ring. I'll have a coffee and talk to Bachelor Number Two.

But it didn't stop ringing. Persistent little bugger, isn't he? I idly started to count the rings. I got fed up at 20, and walked over to pick the damn thing up.

"Yes, hello?" My vocal cords sounded clogged, like an old queen's after a big night on the town.

"Yes, I was interested in your ad in *New York* magazine?"

"Is there something wrong with it?" I asked, not too quick on the uptake at 8:30 Monday morning.

"No, I was wondering, are you available for foot worship?"

Jesus, was I ready for this? "I want you to call me back later," I said, trying to summon the proper stern, dismissive tone. Groggy grandeur was all I could manage.

"Yes, but I was wondering—"

"Good-bye," I said, and hung up. Let him keep on wondering, I thought. A little wonder keeps a person young.

As for me, I was going into the kitchen and splash some hot coffee onto my face.

I got about halfway across the living room before the phone rang again. I answered it, and was about to chew out my foot worshiper for calling back so soon when I realized I was talking to a different person.

This one spent a sputtering minute working up the courage to ask me if I was ready to be served by a cross-dressed male in a French maid's uniform. I wasn't.

By late morning I was sitting on my couch with my arms wrapped around my knees, staring at my phone, its bell disconnected, its red light flashing like a tocsin.

All I could think about was the vast male libido and the army of men who were in thrall to it. It was scaring me. Oh, those humans.

I mean, I had always known that men were generally, as a rule, you know, *ready for it*, but this was something else. This raised the level of their need to crude, exaggerated heights, like a form of mass hysteria you might laugh at in a horror film. The invasion of the body snatchers.

Yes, they were interested. Yes, they would like to make an appointment. Yes, they could come over. How about right now?

At twelve o'clock noon a man walked into my apartment who had called me barely two hours before. What did he do, I thought, wait down at his corner newsstand for fresh, hot copies of the *New York* magazine? What if my ad hadn't appeared? What would he have done to fill up his day?

Let's call him Walter, because he did look a little like Walter Mondale. Bushy, two-tone eyebrows. A long beak nose leading down toward weak, alcoholic lips, watery at the corners. Baggy, puffy eyes that spoke of a habitually one-handed childhood.

Walter kept rising up slightly on the balls of his feet. I thought it was because I was a good foot taller than he was, but then I realized it was simple excitement. Walter was very excited to see me.

"May I say you are extremely beautiful?" he ventured.

I tried to cover up my nervousness by assuming a brisk, business-like attitude.

What did Walter do for a living?

Surprise, surprise, he was in insurance.

And how was the insurance business these days?

Fine, he said. Walter worried about government interference. A tiny lizard tongue retrieved a droplet of liquid that had been glistening at the corner of his lips.

How long had he been interested in role playing and female domination? I was just babbling.

Four years.

Uh-huh. And who else had he seen?

Walter mentioned some names that I did not recognize. Uh-huh, I nodded sagely, as if they were my best friends, and we had spoken often by phone, comparing notes on clients like Walter.

What kind of fantasy was he interested in?

Someone had yelled "bingo!" in the church basement, and Walter rose on the balls of his feet to retrieve his prize.

"Go-go-go-golden sh-sh-showers," he said, spraying the words out, giving himself a little foretaste of what was to come.

A golden shower. He wanted me to piss on him.

Can I do that? I wondered. Luckily, I had been pouring coffee down my throat like a truck driver that whole morning. In fact, I felt like excusing myself and going to the bathroom right at that moment. I recalled Lenny Bruce's definition of a loser as a guy who steps out of a golden shower to take a piss.

So physically, I was Walter's dream date. But could I do it otherwise?

Morally, could I do it? Forget that. Morality was a high school play put on by amateurs for an audience of idiots.

Emotionally, could I do it? No problem. What else was I there for? What had I placed the ad for, if not to retrieve outrageous requests from total strangers and attempt to fulfill them for money?

So, yes, rifling through my psychological index file, I found that I could do it.

"Well, Walter, I charge $200 an hour?" I said it like that, as a question, and even as I did I wondered why I said it at all.

Later on, I would learn to charge $300 for golden showers, because they were special "treats." But I had started out the day thinking that I would charge $75 an hour. The incessant phone calls had jacked the price slowly skyward, like bids at an auction. By the time Walter walked in, I had firmly determined that my price was $150 an hour, not a penny less.

Walter dug into his the pocket of his suitjacket and brought out a thick, oblong wallet. The $20 bills started to tumble out of it and didn't stop until a ten-count later.

That astonished me, and I realized I was going to spend the whole day, at least, and maybe the rest of my life, in a sort of slow-motion state of astonishment. The phone calls astonished me, both their number and their content. Walter Mondale standing in my apartment asking for a golden shower astonished me.

But what astonished me most was that I was actually turning heel and leading Walter into the bathroom.

I've had lovers who were playfully interested in the process of me peeing. One, in particular, used to like to pass his hands under the flow once in a while, just for a kick. He'd always get a dreamy-eyed look in his eyes as he did so.

But this was different. As soon as we got into the rather tight confines of my New York City apartment bathroom, Walter began to disrobe. His body was sallow and unappetizing. A faint aroma of sour coffee and stale cigarettes arose from his flesh.

I was wearing a black Thierry Mugler mini dress, a short bolero jacket and black patent heels. It surprised me to find myself wearing that, since I had tried on practically my whole closet the night before, and vaguely remembered finally deciding on a different outfit.

As I raised my skirt and slipped out of my panties, Walter watched me with bright-eyed interest, like a crow or a monkey watching something shiny.

I had a sudden moment of grammatical uncertainty. Was it, "Lay down in the tub," or "Lie down in the tub"? And me the product of a Coxsackie education. I chose wrong.

"Lay down in the tub," I commanded, although it came out like, "Lay down in the tub?" For some reason, all my statements were still coming out as questions. A sign of irredeemable rookiness.

Walter didn't correct me. He stepped onto the cold porcelain, asserting his footing carefully, like a man who had been warned that most accidents happen in the home.

"I like to see it... as it comes out," he said.

Well, pal, whatever floats your boat, I thought. I wondered if they would all be like this, their requests winging out of the psychological twilight zone like errant boomerangs.

I straddled the sides of the tub in my heels. With Walter there already, there wasn't much room. For a moment I thought I was going to tumble down onto him.

"Where do you—?"

"On my face," Walter said quickly. "On my face."

I straddled him and the deed was done. I looked down and watched the long ribbon of urine twist out of my urethra and splash onto his face.

"Ewwww—ahhhhhh—ewwww, mistress," Walter bleated. His voice took on a curious nasal groan, flattening out comically, as if he were auditioning for a cartoon character. He blinked his eyes spasmodically and flapped his lips. "Ewwwww—ahhhh—ewww, mistress, mistress!"

The pee beaded in fat droplets on my pubic hair. I was holding onto both sides of the tub, and my arms were getting tired. My bladder, however, was coming through for me. It was one world-class bladder. After I die, it's headed to the Golden Shower Hall of Fame.

"You want some more?" I asked.

"Just... just... just..." he stammered. I was surprised that he did not have a full erection when he came.

One of the great things about golden showers, I have since found, is that the clean-up is a snap. I simply turned on the shower, threw in some Lysol, and washed away both my urine and Walter's genetic discharge. He was out of the apartment a quick five minutes later.

By six o'clock that evening, the evening of my first full day as a professional, advertised, golden-shower-giving dominatrix, I had done three sessions back-to-back. Only the first one was a golden shower. Bachelor Number Two wanted latex.

When I explained to him that I wasn't equipped, he suggested we go down to the Noose, an elegant S-M boutique on 19th Street off lower Fifth, and buy some right then and there. On his dime. In the middle of a session, with the meter running. Whatever wets your suit, pal, I said, and off we went on our merry astonished way.

At 6:37 p.m. on the evening of my first full day as a professional, advertised, latex-wearing dominatrix, I had knocked off for the day and was staring at the cobra eye of my telephone indicator light, which was telling me I had an incoming call. I was propped up on my couch with a Stoli martini in my hand, poured from a bottle *which I had ordered in*, for chrissakes, so complete was my sense of triumphant astonishment.

There was $762.50 on the end table next to the insistent telephone. That represented two $200 sessions and one $400 (the latex guy had taken two hours getting me around town and back), minus $37.50 for the Vitamin V delivered straight to my door.

I paid off the *New York* magazine ad in my mind, leaving a $512.50 profit. For one day. And the phone light kept on flashing.

Urine the money, I punned quietly to myself, even though technically that wasn't correct, since only one of the sessions had been a golden shower.

Dear Ms. Sonya:

I have been interested in female supremacy for over 20 years. I have been trained in person by several dominas, of which Ms. Mir (mid-1980's) and Mistress Victoria Cruz (mid-1990) are the most notable.

My interests in female domination run to erotic teasing, sexual arousal coupled with denial of release, shoe and boot fetishes, legs, stockings and garter belts and general sexual control of the male by the Mistress. I also enjoy mild corporal punishment and penile restraint. I am not interested in severe or hard physical punishment or restraint, anything to do with excrement or urine, anything that results in bodily injury or abusive or profane language.

I would like to meet a Mistress that can seriously control my sexual libido and can help me to grow further into my deep need to serve a woman. That need compels me to serve a Mistress, to give that Mistress pleasure (in whatever way she requires) and to be serious and sincere with that Mistress.

I am sure that you hear this often, but there is something captivating about you. Something that drew me to you. Most of the other dominas are without effect on me or, at best, create a physical attraction. There was something else with you.

Sincerely,
Jason R.

So I had officially decided to make my living off of men. It looks bald and a little repugnant when it's put down on the page like that, but actually I have always made my living off of men.

In some sense, of course, all women make their living off of men all the time, since men control the money-making apparatus in the world. Every dollar comes to us already soiled with the grease of men's palms.

There is a South American Indian tribe in which the aristocracy gets high by eating psychedelic mushrooms, and the lower class gets high by waiting outside the pueblo until a member of the privileged classes comes outside to piss. They collect the urine and drink it, getting off on the traces of hallucinogens in the aristocratic pee.

That's men and women. We females get our highs—and everything else—second-hand.

I suppose if you sat down and interpreted my romantic history in a certain way, you could come to the conclusion that I followed a predetermined path into hookerdom. My troubles with men, you'd say, made me into a queen of pain. This relationship plus this relationship yields Mistress Sonya, dominatrix extraordinaire. Feel the sting of lash, worm.

The idea strikes me as old-fashioned, as if any stain on the immaculate purity of woman always comes from man. It's been my experience that women are perfectly capable of wandering off the straight-and-narrow all by themselves.

The shrinks out there can comb this record all they want for evidence of hatred of men. (Isn't it interesting that while "misogyny," hatred of women, is a fairly well-known word, there is no comparable opposite? Especially when the need for one is so clear?)

My direct testimony will be that I have always loved men. But then, direct testimony is suspect, isn't it? One's hidden motives are not always clear even to oneself.

I mark the beginning of my romantic career not with doubtful Thomas (he of the bloody seatcovers at the drive-in movie), but with a tall, gangly, smooth-skinned art student I met in the cafeteria of the Brooklyn Museum.

The Coxsackies of America, the nation's small towns and hamlets, owe a big vote of thanks to New York City and LA. Those two cities alone skim off the majority the misfits, weirdos and troublemakers from all over the country, and thus ensure that small town peace will remain undisturbed.

Of course, no vote of thanks is forthcoming. In fact, the small town mindset regards New York and LA with a poisonous hatred. Which is okay by me, since I bugged out of the burg that had turned my teenage years into a hellish version of *Green Acres*, minus the laugh track.

Like a salmon swimming upstream to its spawning grounds, like a broodmare heading to paddock, like a dog returning unto its vomit, I scraped the dung off my feet and ran back to Brooklyn right after I graduated high school.

I was going to be an artist. I was going to be everything Coxsackie wasn't. Rich, fast, sophisticated, cultured. Eat my dust, dairy girls and boys.

The effect was diminished somewhat by the fact that I was moving into the apartment of my grandparents. Which probably would have caused a laugh back at Coxsackie High, where I had breezily assured everyone I was going to live in a garden apartment in the middle of the Greenwich Village. "Where?" was their response. Joan was right. I was wasted on them.

I was 17. A young 17, not an urban 17. My height had come in the last few years of high school, and I finally topped out at six feet—"a model's height," Joan told me, proud of her daughter. I inherited her good bone structure, also—the cheekbones that were like a couple of karate chops to men's hearts—as well as her ample, almost old-fashioned hourglass figure.

But I was having none of that. I wanted to be gaunt, skeletal, a ghost. I wanted to be a black-clad wraith out of Baudelaire, or at least out of Allen Ginsberg, with dark rings beneath my eyes to show that I Had Lived. I tossed out all my old clothes (the stench of Coxsackie still hung on them) and haunted "Sally's"—the Salvation Army thrift stores—for my couture.

Being folks from the Old Country, my grandparents thought I was insane. What had happened to their little girl? May and Wally looked on in baffled disbelief as I completed my transformation from rube to bohemian.

As Dolly Parton used to say, looking this cheap costs a lot of money, and one of the main arguments around the apartment in those days was my grandparents' refusal to bankroll my downwardly mobile lifestyle. I thought they were money-grubbing, tight-assed and stingy. They thought I was a prodigal daughter ruined by the pipe-dreams of the counter-culture.

My ostensible reason for being in Brooklyn was to attend Pratt Institute, an island of artistic pretension floating in the tenement sea of Bedford-Stuyvesant. I was signed up for painting and printmaking, but I told myself that the only subject worthy of study was Life Itself.

This I applied myself to with an energy and recklessness that, looking back on it, astounds me. If only somebody had clued me in, or at the very least slipped a couple of downers into my drink to slow me down.

Nobody did, so at Pratt I embarked on a campaign to dismantle every trace of small-town, bourgeois, oh-so-conventional thinking I had left in my psyche. I realize now that this was an oh-so-conventional approach to the situation I was in, but back then I thought I was a firebrand.

The students around me were shriekingly competitive. Most of them came from New York City, and were used to drawing blood every morning just fighting for a seat on the subway. They were thus well prepared for atmosphere at Pratt, which was one of a long, mad scramble up the slippery slope of Art.

But art was, as they say, abstract. The more immediate goal was worldly success, meaning members of the opposite sex would go down on you at a wave of a paintbrush. Everywhere you went in the halls of Pratt you could imagine the sound of long knives being sharpened, as classmates prepared to decorate each other with dorsal puncture wounds.

Occasionally, however, a pair of us would manage to retract our claws long enough to mate. When I saw hollow-eyed art boys joined at the hip with their ragingly sexy girlfriends, I decided this was the last word in cool. I had to get one myself.

His name was Andrés Serrano, and he would later inflame the passions of Senator Jesse Helms by inserting a crucifix in a beaker of his own urine, calling the resulting *objet* "Piss Christ." He would effectively bring down the whole National Endowment of the Arts, forcing the question of government subsidy of the arts onto the national political agenda.

That was ahead of him, of course. Back when I knew him, he was just a skinny Hispanic with a wardrobe that knew one color only, black. Andrés was on scholarship to the Brooklyn Museum School of Art. This forged in him a bitterly envious hatred of the rich kids at Pratt. I was surprised, although I shouldn't have been, that he even consented to go out with me after he realized I was one of the hated Pratt brats.

His sullen art-student pose was mitigated by the fact that he still lived with his mother on Lorimer Street in Greenpoint. He was tall, with an alfalfa-sprout stubble and a heavy, self-serious brow—he liked to think his look was after Marcel Duchamp.

I thought Andrés was marvelous, especially after I brought him back to May and Wally's and my grandfather yelled at me to—and I quote—"Get that bloody P.R. out of my house." Andrés sulked for a week. Later he made it a point to tell me that his father was Honduran, not Puerto Rican.

Our relationship was not overly physical. Like a lot of city kids, we didn't have any place to go to screw. Besides, Andrés's angst prevented him from being too frisky—he was thinking so much that his brain didn't have any blood to lend his cock.

But using Andrés as a willing co-conspirator, I educated myself in the fine art of the blowjob behind the statues and bushes of Grand Army Plaza. Thus I can honestly say I did learn an art in art school.

He wrote poetry and took himself seriously. We made art together. He blew up a bunch of huge beach balls and I painted them black. "Black Balls," he called it. Come to think of it, Jesse Helms would probably be even more horrified about that concept than he was over Piss Christ.

You only get one first big romance in life. Looking back on it, I can't quite put my finger on how it all fell apart. There was no one event, no blowout argument or tearful leavetaking that I remember. It was more modern than that. I just recall a sense of cluttered, chaotic lives, and that we somehow misplaced each other. Not with a bang but a whimper.

But what were we going to do? Marry one another? Move to Great Neck and raise a family? Andrés had things to do, art to make, U.S. senators to offend. And I had many miles to go before I took my last Valium.

But the first cut is the deepest. I don't exactly think of him every time I piss or see a crucifix. Maybe every time I see a black beach ball. With just a whiff of sadness, the sadness every one of us has, except those Barbie and Kens who marry out of high school, the sadness that makes us into that strange animal, the adult human.

For some odd reason, once I embarked upon the path of the professional dominatrix, once my phone started ringing and I did those first few sessions and felt the warm glow of all those hundred-dollar bills in my hand, I suddenly got cold feet.

It can't be this easy, I thought. I have to be doing something wrong.

I tried not to let it bother me, and concentrated on getting my apartment in some kind of shape so that it could accommodate both my business and my living quarters without too much overlap. I emptied out one end of my living room and set up my "home office" there.

Like I said, I don't believe in elaborate dungeons. Despite admiring Willie's incredible basement room, I wanted to keep mine simple. Through repeated visits to the Noose, to the hardware store and the lumber yard, my little slave's paradise came together.

I knew what I wanted, but at the same time I was worried I was doing something wrong. I didn't trust my instincts. Next to the huge leather-and-rack dungeons of the major houses, my loft looked forlorn. Maybe I was just kidding myself. Maybe I wasn't a natural at this at all.

An element of doubt crept into the proceedings. In any elaborate charade such as female domination, self-consciousness is what in today's parlance is called a "buzz-kill." The dominatrix must maintain the illusion of certainty at all costs.

I remember being in the middle of a session with a man I'll call Marvin, a foot worshiper. I was dressed in an outrageously vampy Lycra dress with a sheer powernet inset. It was all wasted on my slave, for whom I essentially disappeared from the ankle up. The rest of my body was simply a support system for my feet.

Bootlickers are some of the most monomaniacal of all fetishists. I had one guy who sliced his erotic pie so thin he could get off on moccasins, and moccasins only.

"Would you like the stilettos, or the mules?" I asked Marvin, a little distracted.

I saw a cloud pass over his face, which was otherwise lit by the bright sun of the Look. "What would *you* like, Mistress?" he asked plaintively, and I realized I had violated the rigid code dictating our relationship.

I must tell him what I want, not ask him. I had to cram my choice of heel down his throat, snap it off and choke him with it. Then maybe he would go home happy.

But the mood was broken, and the session ran to a bumpy, unsatisfactory end. My own doubt had polluted the proceedings.

Afterwards, as I was absently cleaning Marvin's spittle from my heels, I decided I had gone at the whole project all wrong. I should have apprenticed myself to an established dominatrix, learned the licks, so to speak, and then gone on to build my own reputation and clientele.

I would have to backtrack. I needed a mentor. In this case, a mentrix. I found a notice for the "Ava Taurel Institute," which promised state-of-the-art, scientific domination of the male by the female.

I called the number and bluffed my way into an appointment with Ava herself, saying I was an experienced dominatrix seeking employment. Which was all true, if one is allowed to expand the definition of "experienced" to include my own personal Walter Mondale, Marvin the bootlicker, Italian Willie and a handful of others.

Taurel's "institute" (S-M bordellos compete with each to evoke the most outlandish name possible, from institute to "salon," "chateau," "academy," even—for a place in the Bay Area—"church") was a floor of a professional building in Midtown, on West 56th Street.

Unwittingly, I made a couple of mistakes right from the beginning of my relationship with Mistress Ava. Number one, I innocently asked the doorman where the Taurel Institute was. A big no-no, given the secrecy and mystery that Taurel tries to project, as well as the fact that her landlords may not know what it is, specifically, that draws so many men to her door.

Number two was the way I dressed, in a black-and-white Versace suit with a short tailored skirt.

"What do you think you're doing?" Taurel shouted at me, as soon as I entered her "office." No hellos, no handshakes, just what-do-you-think-you're-doing?

I was dressed like a hooker, she said. Totally unacceptable, she said. Give the place a bad rep with the doorman. Had I talked to the him on the way up? I had? Had I mentioned Ava Taurel? I had? Very bad, very, very bad. It was as if she was scolding a dog. I expected her to take out a ruler and rap my knuckles.

Taurel is a short, chunky woman who always looks to me like she needs a good scrubbing. I have since learned that her surly attitude is a common occupational hazard for working dominatrices. They have a tragic tendency to stay in character even after the whistle blows and it's time to knock off.

It's almost a parody of the public perception of S-M. As a rule, dominatrices are surly, loud, grating, annoying, rude, abrupt, ill-mannered. They are harridans and termagants, a couple of five-dollar words which are covered on the male side of things by the convenient catch-all phrase of bitch.

Of course, dominatrices are paid to be that way, but who asks them to take their work home with them? Learn to give it a rest, ladies, please!

A lot of this excess attitude comes from the rather shaky standing that the dominatrix enjoys vis-a-vis the rest of society. It puts her on the defensive.

Ava Taurel, for example, was terrified of getting tossed out of her institute on her ear by a rampaging landlord. This forced her into an adversarial pose, which she articulated by shrieking like a crazy woman at me, a neophyte who had just wandered through her door.

She was squat and thick next to my more zoftig, shall we say Rubenesque, frame. *Dumpy* would be an apt adjective for her, in her ideas, as it turned out, as in her looks.

Brittle, salt-and-pepper hair. Cut short but not cropped, more like a modified bob. Not at all well-endowed in the good looks department, a fact which I think she tries to compensate for by projecting what she considers to be a regal demeanor.

Ava Taurel takes herself very seriously.

I found this out when I sat before her, having already had my ears pinned back within the first few seconds of meeting her. I sketched out what my experience had been, over the past two weeks, running my own makeshift S-M house of pain.

"Not that it really qualifies as a house," I said, joking. "Maybe a cottage of pain."

Cottage industry, cottage of pain. Very clever, if I did think so myself. I laughed. Ava Taurel did not. In fact, in all the short time I knew her, she never emitted anything that could have been construed as a chuckle, a giggle or a guffaw.

I tried a different tack, describing some of my clients. "You know, the oddest thing, I can't shake the feeling that they are the ones who are calling all the shots. I mean, they're telling me what they want, right? So it turns out they're the dominant ones!"

My astonishment at this fact, which was just then coming home to me, caused me to laugh some more.

"This is funny to you?" Ava Taurel said. She had a slightly skewed Bavarian-Hungarian accent, the kind you can send away for, although in her case it was evidently real enough, the product of an imperfect sloughing off of the homeland.

She explained that my slaves seemed in charge only because I was not controlling my sessions to the ultimate degree possible. In her clipped, curt tones, she said she would show me what she meant.

For all her imperious bearing, Ava Taurel had decorated her "office," with a nappy sort of cheesiness that I remember being totally unimpressed by, cheap and tacky as it was. But perhaps she was saving her real push for her dungeon, I thought, as she stepped forward to lead me into the next room.

It was not so. The space was an unadorned rectangle, painted flat black, devoid of artifice or design. I recalled Willie's basement dungeon, and how it made me feel when I entered it. Ava Taurel's institute suffered in comparison.

It took my eyes a little while to adjust to the dimly lit room, and my ears a while to shut out the Germanic chatter of Mistress Ava (once she started talking, she really kept it up). I realized with a start that there was a session going on.

Two dominatrices were present, one a charmingly sweet young thing dressed in a white lace bustier, the other a stiffer older woman, outfitted in leather and cut of the Ava Taurel mold. They were working over a male who was on his hands and knees in one corner.

"Heel!" the stiff one was barking, and the male would gamely try to walk beside her. He was hampered in this

endeavor by the fact that his penis was leashed by the most
elaborate macramé of knots I had ever seen. The poor tool
was tied every which way but loose, engorged and empurpled
by the relentless constriction that occurred each time the rope
was pulled.

I could see that the two of them were working him in
tandem. Mistress Sweetness and Light would stand in front of
the slave, presenting her vision of loveliness to him, making
him lunge forward after it. Mistress Stiff would yank him
back to her side every time he strayed an inch too far. An S-M
variation of carrot and stick, good cop/bad cop. Twice as
expensive, too.

"Now, whom do you think is in control here?" Ava Taurel
demanded. Actually, I had my own ideas, but I kept silent.
"He'll have blisters on his penis when they get through with
him."

The room smelled faintly of Crisco. There were large blue
glass jars filled with plastic gloves.

"Tighter, tighter," groaned the slave, and then all of a
sudden I recognized him.

He was a leading player in a daytime soap opera, a gorgeous hunk adored by probably half the female population of
the U.S. Ava Taurel watched the slow dawning cross my face
with immense satisfaction. She had scheduled our interview
herself, so she must have known Mister Daytime Ratings was
going to be there. She had trotted out her star pupil to
impress me.

Mistress Stiff cinched her leash a couple notches deeper
into the man's flesh. "He'll have blisters on his penis..." I real-

ized the institute was the kind of place where sex organs are called by their formal names.

Suddenly the soap opera hunk looked past his carrot and saw me. He got a look of inexpressible longing on his face and his front paws crashed out from under him. His face hit the rug, but he managed to crane up and stare at me, groaning.

"Swine!" Mistress Stiff shrieked. She turned to Ava. "Mistress Ava, James has ejaculated upon the rug." Ejaculated. With his penis, no doubt.

This was not allowed. No coming upon the rug at the Institute. Slaves must work their pathetic dinks in the dressing rooms, or elsewhere.

"Do you think we want to see your disgusting jism? We do not want to see your disgusting jism at all!" Mistress Sweet was shouting down into the actor's face, but the poor man had come, so the dynamic was pretty empty. The thrill was gone. He just wanted to be untied and allowed to go home and memorize the next day's scripts.

Ava and I walked back into her office. "Oh, you have so much to learn," she said to me, pity brimming in her voice.

Hardly worth the effort it would take to teach me, I thought. I had seen all too clearly what had happened in that dungeon. I had inspired her slave simply by being there. It gave me a surge of new confidence.

For some reason, my look, my aura, my *gestalt* was like balm in Gilead for the submissive male. It's like a high school fantasy of female power. I walk into the room and they climax.

"I don't really need a new employee," Ava Taurel was saying to me. Penis, ejaculate, employee—formal nomenclature only, please. "But you do have a commanding presence."

She told me to come back the following day, but I was listening with only half an ear. I realized that I didn't need Ava Taurel or anyone else. Bitches? We don't need no fucking bitches...

I was a natural. Me, Babe Ruth and Ben Hogan. We only come this way every so often, so the most should be made of us when we do.

Ava was already looking at me possessively. I knew I would make an enemy if I didn't come back and work for her. But what was she going to do, blackball me? You'll never crack a whip in this town again.

I told her I would think seriously about coming to work for her, and left her to her Crisco funk and blue jars of protection.

When I got home, my phone was ringing.

Dear Sonya,

My name is T_____ L_____ and I am a SWM age 30, 5'9", 150 lbs, muscular build, brown hair and blue eyes. I smoke but I don't drink or take drugs. I would love to be allowed the pleasure of receiving some "DIVINE AND ELEGANT DOMINATION" from you.

While I am a novice at B & D, I have known for several years that I am submissive and feel that it is time I sought out the help of a professional. I have been very unlucky in my quest to find a girlfriend that will help me satisfy my submissive desires. They all think I am some sort of a pervert when I tell them of my fantasy to be tied up and dominated by a beautiful woman!

As far as my fantasies and fetishes go, I have a foot fetish, this includes all types of high heeled shoes and boots as well as bare and stocking feet. I enjoy pantyhose as well as stockings.

I find leather and latex clothing (especially the smell of leather) very arousing also. I have never been spanked or whipped, but I would be interested in giving it a try so long as it is on the mild side. Being bound helpless and forced to lick your high heels or whatever would also be interesting. I am also slightly interested in forced cross-dressing.

I look forward to hearing from you.

Sincerely,
T.L.

What were we thinking?

In retrospect that crazy period of the late Sixties and early Seventies may have taken on a roseate glow, with adjectives like "idealistic" and "ecstatic" thrown around by glib tongues and facile minds. We Baby Boomers enjoy the smug certainty that the Sixties represented the Best Years of Our Lives. But somewhere underneath all that lies the question.

What were we thinking? What the hell did we think life was, that we could play at it like a game?

It all seemed logical at the time. Or, if not logical, then at least inevitable. That I would take up with a woman-beating black man and skip off with him to the rain forest. Tra la la. Let's blame it on the drugs.

All I know is that once my relationship with Andrés Serrano fell apart, I still wasn't finished with my elaborate rejection of my Coxsackie past. I was still evolving, as they used to say. Evolving right out of my fucking mind.

I took a path that a lot of women did, to declare themselves free of their parents, free of their straightlaced backgrounds and finally, free of their old selves. I had an affair with a black man. A torrid, two-year-long affair.

I've since been told that this is almost a cliché of lefty-liberal development. Ask a lot of lesbians, for example, how they got to where they are, and a majority will say their sexual development went something like this: nightmare high school, men of color in college, out of the closet afterwards.

It's like a trigger mechanism to jettison old beliefs, old baggage. Uptight America has made fucking a black into crossing some sort of emotional Rubicon. Once black, you never turn back, because they won't let you.

His name was Eugene Monroe. He was a professor at Brooklyn's Pratt Institute, and he made quite a career of snagging young nubiles such as myself, no doubt in order to facilitate their politico-socio-sexual dawning. I suppose that this would be construed as some sort of sexual harassment nowadays, because, after all, Eugene was in some sort of position of authority, and his targets were always young students.

But who was using whom? He was getting his ya-yas off, but I was doing something I most devoutly wished to be doing. I was shaking the dust of Coxsackie out of my soul.

For a long time I thought the sun shone out of Gene Monroe's ass. He was the total antithesis of everything that I had known in the first 17 years of my life. He was like a god of Otherness.

I remember when I first saw him, at a Pratt party in October on a rooftop overlooking Bedford-Stuyvesant, the worst ghetto on the Eastern seaboard. If there was any justice, the whole vista would have been in flames and the bullets would have been nailing our lily-white asses one by one.

Instead, I saw this magisterial black man hanging out near the food table (Gene was a masterful freeloader), wearing a pair of paint-spattered pants that were like Joseph's coat of many colors.

I immediately looked down at my own jeans. They had a few smears of Cadium red on them, some dabs of blue and green. Also some black paint stains I had added myself, seeking to balance things out and show that I dealt in the colors of darkness.

I was inordinately proud of those jeans. I wore them until May physically attempted to take them away to wash them.

"You're gonna stink?" she shouted. "You want to stink like a bum?"

Well, yes, that is exactly what I did want to do. I had almost subconsciously drifted into a competition with the rest of the Pratt painting students, to see who could have the Hippest Pair of Paint-Spattered Jeans.

As soon as I saw Gene, I realized we were not even in the running. His jeans were awesome. They spoke of years of artistic suffering, pursuit of the muse, canvasses propped up in chilly lofts with good northern light. Jackson fucking Pollack learned everything he knew from those jeans.

So I did what any young painting student had to do when confronted with those jeans. I fell in love. Later on, too late, I realized that Gene's jeans were merely part of a strategy to get me out of my own. He used to prop his jeans up in his closet and only take them out for special occasions, when he was on the prowl.

"Hello there," he said, suddenly materializing next to me. His voice was smooth and mellow, in contradiction to his fierce appearance. I proceeded to choke on my drink in a spectacular display of uncoolness.

Gene ignored my discombobulation. "You're the one doing oils." I had tried to distinguish myself from the herd at Pratt by an uncompromising allegiance to oil paint, while so many of my peers were wallowing in acrylics.

Oils were brutally unforgiving, and I was having a lot of trouble, but I was adamant.

Yes, I was the one doing oils, I simpered. I was so thankful that El Monroe, Icon of Cool, had deigned to notice me that I nearly swooned.

"Oils are bullshit," He Who Possessed the Jeans intoned. "All those old dago cats, you know, totally out. You got to get up with it. The new stuff they're doing with synthetics is wild, man. Why don't you take my class?"

I took his class, and Gene took me, totally, body and soul. The small matter of his wife and two children did not stop me. I moved into his studio, stopped going to school altogether. I was content with being Mrs. Gene Monroe—the *real* Mrs. Gene Monroe—a stand-by-your-man woman, fetching my master's slippers and cigarettes and beer.

We made a good pair. He was tall and bronze; I was blonde, long-limbed, the perfect birch to grow in the shadow of his mighty oak.

I only thought I was content. It slowly crept up on me that Gene drank, and when he drank he treated me to spittle-flinging streams of verbal abuse I can still hear ringing in my ears even today.

It was the first time I ever felt the hand of man strike me. At the time, I thought he might be right, that I might indeed be a street-tramp whore with a gutter for a mouth and a hatred for the black man that rivaled the Klan's.

Things began to spiral down for us, for me. I can pin the beginning of a long period of endless parties, wasted nights, hungover noons on that relationship with Gene Monroe. Everyone was doing it, letting their life roll by on alkaloid wheels, drinking too much, partying too much.

"When I work hard, I play hard," Gene used to say to me, but it always seemed he was neglecting the first part of that formula.

We tried to outrun our doom by splitting the States and moving to Costa Rica. He got a grant from the enlightened liberal administration of Mayor John Lindsay ("a cocksucking honky" according to Gene) and promptly bought a used Land Rover with it. He actually believed his own rants about the racist administration at Pratt enough to resign. (At least, that's what he told me. Later I found he had merely taken a sabbatical.)

We drove out from New York City on New Year's Day, January 1973. The snow on the ground was shredded and gray, but I tried to tell myself it was something out of *Dr. Zhivago*, and Omar Sharif was riding a white stallion across the steppes to shack up with Julie Christie.

A tawdry little racist incident at a Howard Johnson's in Phoenix sobered me up a little. The clerk there refused to seat us in the restaurant.

Gene's response was to go on a whiskey binge that lasted until we crossed the border to Mexico at Nogales. Then he switched to tequila.

Costa Rica was paradise, but it turns out that living in paradise doesn't mean your life won't be hell. There was too much history that we brought along with us, too much enervating sun, too much good dope. We had dropped off the edge of the world into a cannabis haze.

Gene was a devotee of Buckminster Fuller. He wanted to build a geodesic dome and hide out in the hinterlands. We wound up in Cahuita, on the Caribbean coast, near the Panamanian border, where he bought six hectares of beach land for $150.

Cahuita was in the most undeveloped part of a unevenly developed Third World country. The road north to Limon, the nearest city with an airport, was still dirt. We were in the boonies, and when you are in the boonies of a Third World country, you're out there.

Cahuita had a large Creole population and many of the natives spoke an English-Creole patois, confusing to us in that "All right!" meant "hello" and "okay" meant "good-bye."

Perhaps the lingo would have been easier to figure out if our minds weren't thwarted by a jungle pharmacopoeia of drugs.

Gene drank poisonous rum called Quaro brewed by the locals. When he was stoned, he would shoot parrots and monkeys out of the rain forest canopy with an ancient .22, cackling like an idiot. I ate mangoes and concentrated on trying to survive. I half expected Gene to turn the gun on me. Every once in a while, he would be sitting on the verandah of our tin-roof-on-sticks, and in mid-sentence abruptly get up and walk away into the rain forest. He would not come back for days.

"You really are a world-class, king-size bitch, you know that?" He said it so often that I began to believe it.

"You're just finding that out now?" I would say airily, putting my best face on it.

"You have the blood of the devil flowing in your veins." He stared at me, bloodshot eyes set off nicely by his gray pallor. "Maybe I should bleed you. Let it out."

"Yes, maybe you could paint with it." Gene wasn't painting. It was a sore spot for him.

"Fuck you and the jackass you rode in on."

"That would be you, wouldn't it?"

I was keeping it light, but I was actually terrified. I wasn't quite sure if it was only rhetoric with Gene. For all I knew, he was planning his own little personal Jonestown there in the jungles of Costa Rica.

It is incredible to me that I lasted as long as I did. I was sick all the time. In Costa Rica, the parasites enter the body through the soles of the feet, worming their microscopic way through your skin and into your bowels. I read somewhere there is a phobia that represents the fear of air. I developed the next most basic fear. I became afraid of walking.

A year after I arrived, I hitched a ride to Limon and wired Joan for the money I needed to go home. I couldn't find Gene to say good-bye. I crawled back to Coxsackie with my tail between my legs and an intestinal parasite eating at my guts like a guilty conscience.

Round one of Sonya Versus the World had gone to the world by unanimous decision.

Let us now praise famous submissive men.

Soon after my abortive audition with Ava Taurel, I serviced a series of clients whose names would be eminently recognizable to readers of supermarket tabloids everywhere. That I was able to successfully answer the needs of these celebrities increased my confidence further. It confirmed my belief that I had no reason to seek outside help or instruction, from Ava or from anybody.

The famous are different from you and I—they are more widely known. But it's good to remember they are also just people, a fact that gets lost in the frenzy of celebrity worship that goes on in America today.

The rich and famous so beloved by Robin Leach are endowed with the same hive of anxieties as the rest of us, the same biological urgencies and embarrassingly human foibles.

Probably more, because the famous are so often driven and compulsive people.

You've probably all heard stories of the wide submissive streak running down the back of James Dean. Nicknamed "The Human Ashtray," Jimmy was almost as tortured in real life as the characters he played up on the screen.

"You're tearing me apart!" Dean wails in *Rebel Without a Cause*, and that line could serve as a battle cry (and an open invitation) for submissives the world over.

I knew in theory that celebrities were just as likely to be kinked up as anyone else. So I really should not have been surprised at what I found when I was summoned one evening to a midtown hotel. I was told to dress conservatively to get by security. I was directed to a specific room.

I had done a few "outcalls" previously—the kind of session where I went to the client, usually to his hotel. I tended to avoid them, because I could not control the situation on the other end. But if the client was calling from a reputable hotel, I felt reassured. And this man's voice had been so soothing and sonorous on the phone that I agreed immediately to come to him.

My encounter with him began in the same way as those few times when I did outcalls before. I breezed through the lobby of the deluxe Midtown hotel, wearing a gray wool, very conservative Calvin Klein business suit, so as not to attract attention.

Hotel house dicks love to hassle prostitutes. It adds some glamour to what is essentially a menial rent-a-cop job. They stand at the portals of New York's most upscale hostelries, vetting each passing woman for telltale signs that she might be a working girl. Then they get huge hardons hassling the ones they find, shaking them down for free blowjobs or pawing them over as they toss them out on the street.

So the call girls dress conservatively when they get summoned to a Midtown hotel by visiting businessmen. In this endless game of cat-and-mouse, hotel bars are also famous for the action between the house dicks and the girls who try to avoid them.

The security guys are always fucking up and accosting some innocent woman who they only think is a hooker. One couple won a million dollar damage suit against a hotel for being detained and questioned by its security force (the man was black, the woman was white).

I successfully negotiated the gauntlet in the lobby and proceeded upstairs. Like I said, it all started out like an ordinary outcall session. But I feel like I should almost have expected it when the door to hotel room opened and there stood an Oscar-winning actor whose name is...

Yes, well. I won't tell his name. For a couple of reasons.

One is that there are people who don't believe that the process of "outing" is a good idea. I suppose there's been some cases where it's necessary, as with a Bush cabinet staffer, say, working for an administration that consistently supported anti-gay sentiment. The hypocrisy of that is so vomitous it requires some response.

But beyond that, and all arguments to the contrary, outing seems only to answer the natural human need to gossip about our fellows. It's not that the gossip instinct is in any way blameworthy—I read every gossip column known to man, so I can't say that. It's just that the right to privacy far outweighs it.

The other reason I won't name names among my clients is that mine is a business which depends on privacy. Discretion is the better part of my income. Until that unimaginable millennium when all forms of human sexuality are accepted for what they are, commonplace and normal, instead of seen as freakish perversions to be ridiculed and judged, then the clients who bring their special needs to me shall remain nameless.

(Of course, for some masochists, the absolute height of pleasure would consist of being exposed in front of the whole world. They would writhe, paroxysms of guilt and shame coursing through their bodies like jolts of alternating current. They would bear the laughter and insults like so many caresses. But then they would be in the same position as the old vaudevillian who commits suicide as a stage act. What would they for an encore?)

Most of my clients fear nothing more than being outed. They remind me of scared white rabbits, venturing from their burrows and wandering into a wolf-den. They blink in the harsh bright light of another human being's presence, and the only way they can stand even my gaze is to internalize me in their own private fairy tale.

Face it, being a submissive is not the most glamorous form of sexual fetishism. "Hi, my name is Dennis and I like to lick women's boots." The natural human response to this is a hearty, "Well, get over it, pal!"

So their identities shall be safe with me.

We'll call this client Oscar, in honor of his Academy Award. He seemed genuinely annoyed that I recognized him and was in the process of overreacting to his celebrity. I'm reminded of a story they tell about Charlie Chaplin and a young star-struck girl he had seduced. In the middle of their lovemaking, she interrupts him mid-thrust to ask, "Mister Chaplin, after this is over, could I have your autograph?"

At least I wasn't that gauche. I recovered quickly, picked up my jaw from where it was rolling around on the floor, and proceeded to business. No further indication was given by me that this man had one of the most widely-known faces in the world. My expression did not betray what I was thinking, which was that I was in the same room with a matinee idol whose mere presence would send half of female America into a swoon.

What did Oscar want?

"Nothing too rough," he said briskly, his initial annoyance with me vanishing as soon as he realized I was going to play it straight, and not whip out a pen and a piece of paper ("It's for my niece, could you just sign it, 'For the cutest li'l rascal'?...")

Basically, what Oscar wanted was a large dildo crammed up his can. He had brought the dingus with him, a beautiful solid ivory model that he took out of a velvet drawstring bag. It looked thick and wicked.

"Never leave home without it," Oscar said, smiling wanly. The thing surprised me, because I had him pegged right away as a bondage sort of guy.

"What do you have on underneath?" he asked. "Ah, perfect, perfect." It was a Victorian spoon corset, black silk set off with antique black lace. Of a type of construction they call "fully boned," believe you me. My breasts were fringed with antique black lace, and my waist was cinched six inches smaller than my normal measurements. Yabba-dabba-do. The thing cost me $250, but seeing the glint in Oscar's Oscar-winning eyes, I figured it was worth it.

With no more ado Oscar shucked his bathrobe and flopped face down across the California King (one size up from a mere King-sized mattress) that he had in the suite. I stood there contemplating that famous ass, the mere glimpse of which had caused gasps of girlish approval in darkened cinemas the country over.

To me, right at that moment, his shanks looked withered and old. "Do you want... lubrication?" I asked, picking up the ivory probe.

"No, thanks," Oscar said cheerfully.

I climbed up on the bed, which actually was roughly the size of California. I experienced a sudden twinge of sadness. I could never see this man's movies again in quite the same way. When my girlfriends dished his handsome good looks I would now have to remain silent. Another stone idol revealed to have a butthole of clay.

"How do you...?" I wondered if I should straddle him.

"That's fine," he said, flexing his ass-cheeks once or twice.

Out of respect for his accomplishments, I was about to apply a little of my spit to the dildo (keeping it clear of my mouth, of course), but he stopped me.

"No need," he said. "Just shove it in."

"Shove it in?"

"Shove it in."

So I did. At first it seemed to have no affect on him at all. As I worked the smooth cylinder in and out of his asshole, however, his breathing became markedly heavier. I played my mind over the leading ladies that Oscar had sex scenes with, had faked it with.

Well, he wasn't faking it with me. I grabbed the dildo with my fist and began hammering it into his rectum. Oscar squirmed his thighs against the bed.

His face was buried in the pillow in front of him, so I couldn't understand why it mattered to him what I was wearing. But occasionally he peered around at me like an aroused goose.

I fisted the dildo into him savagely. You're tearing me apart! When he came, he bucked so hard I thought he was going to pitch me off the bed.

Most men, I would say the majority of the men I see, prefer to slink away after orgasm like shamed gladiators. Either that, or they are rushed and condescending.

The sadness after coitus is well remarked upon, of course. According to the old Roman epigram, it is felt by everyone except women and roosters. And any frat boy will define eternity for you as the time between the man coming and the woman going.

It pleased me that Oscar was not this way at all. He seemed to be that rare man who had accepted his sexuality, even though his particular brand was not the most ordinary.

After his climax he was relaxed and chatty, without any shame that I could perceive. A little aloof, perhaps, with some private self that remained untouchable, but that was just the inevitable byproduct of fame.

He waddled into the bathroom and shat the dildo out into the bathtub, where it ricocheted against the porcelain with a resounding clang. It was all I could do not to burst out laughing, but he did it smoothly and with no self-consciousness, and managed to make even that outlandishly awkward act seem suave.

We even had some mindless conversation, me sitting on his bed in my ridiculous Victorian corset (it only seemed ridiculous then, whereas before it had seemed sexy and alluring), he wrapped in a towel around his waist and sipping a glass of water. He patted my shoulder affectionately as I left, gave me a peck on the cheek and a healthy bonus.

"See you, dearie," he said.

"Call me anytime after one," I said. It was my standard line whenever I liked a client and wanted to see him again.

May 24, 1993

Dear Mistress Sonya,

i am on my knees as i write You this letter, begging to serve You Goddess in any way that pleases You. Although i am only a novice slave, i am also a devoted slave. i understand that my place is at Your feet. i will do Your bidding and serve Your every whim given the chance.

My interests include forced crossdressing and feminization, spiked heel and boot worship, teasing and tormenting, strict bondage, maid service, doggy training and all forms of humiliation.

i would like to share my fantasy with You Mistress. Only You have the power and control to make it a reality. i will do as You command.

Your door opens. Your elegant black leathered hand reaches out and briskly leads me inside. You're wearing a skin-hugging black leather cat suit, mask and thigh-high stiletto-heeled boots. Your power overwhelms me and i immediately drop to my knees.

Mistress fastens a studded collar to my neck and padlocks a black rawhide leash to it, leading me to Your Dungeon. Inside are wooden stocks, a suspension bar, leather covered stretching table and manacles hanging on chains from a wall.

A tug on my leash forces me to follow You to a far corner of the room. As You recline on Your Throne, You pull on my leash and order me to kiss Your boots. Kneeling, i lick one boot from toe to heel, sucking softly at the pointed heel, then lapping the inside of Your ankle to Your hips before repeating the ritual on Your other boot. As i dare to lick above the top of Your boot, you order me to takes my clothes off in the back cell.

You force me to crossdress. As i pull sheer seamed hose up my legs You see how excited i am. With each article of fetish attire—silk garter belt, satin panties, push-up bra with falsies, 8" spiked heels—i become more erect. Your gloved hand squeezes my over-sized clitty and balls and i immediately go limp. You apply the gates of hell. To complete my transformation You apply makeup to my face and a curly blonde wig to my head.

You motion me to a sturdy-looking stock where you imprison my neck and wrists in padded leather as the hinged top is swung closed and locked. my ankles are then fitted with wide leather bracelets and secured to each end of a long steel pipe to keep my legs wide apart. i am helpless.

You brush a gloved hand along my back from neck to ass, squeezing one bun, and positioning Yourself behind me, pressing softly Your leather-clad thighs and pelvis onto my slave rump.

Your hands reach around to my knees, glide up my thighs, hips, stomach and dwell at my nipples. You squeeze and pull, pinch my nipples harder and smack my ass with both hands. You strap on Your harness and slap my face with Your 8" cock. You force me to suck it.

You blindfold me and apply tit clamps. my cries are muffled by a large rubber ball-gag inserted into my mouth and fastened securely to my neck. You say, "slave michael, you are My little slut and so I shall treat you as one." As i feel You apply lubricant to my hole i moan with apprehension and anticipation. As i feel the head of the large leather dildo enter my body, my mind feels only the pain and pleasure that You permit me to experience, Mistress Sonya.

The next sound I hear is the swishing and impact of my Mistress's whip on my back.

i, slave michael, submissively apply for a position (on my knees) as Your personal slave, Mistress Sonya.

Sincerely,
Michael

had tried doing things my own way, and had failed miserably. Back in Coxsackie after the disaster of Costa Rica, my mother convinced me to try things her way for a change.

I would be "rehabilitated." She would bankroll a move back to the city, she said, and make some introductions in the Garment District. The only thing I had to do was to leave bohemia behind.

I didn't have much choice. The tropical microbes doing a dance in my guts did what years of dieting and successive scripts of amphetamines had never accomplished. They made me thin. Emaciated, as a matter of fact. The first thing Joanie did when she saw me was take me to the hospital.

By the time I got well, the thick, ragweed atmosphere of Coxsackie was already beginning to suffocate me. I had to get out. It was like I was in a time machine that kept on making the wrong stops. Help, Mr. Wizard, I don't want to be a dairymaid anymore!

When I got back to the City, I did what any self-respecting woman of that day did when she had a new, deliciously slim figure and no visible means of support. I got a job as a Playboy bunny, at the club just off 5th Avenue down the street from the Plaza and the Pierre.

It was the most ridiculous work I've ever done, and I speak as a woman who sometimes makes her living urinating on men's faces. The bunny-ear outfit, the "rabbit perch"—an awkward, body-contorting maneuver we were supposed to accomplish whenever we approached a table to deliver drinks—the heavy-handed *in loco parentis* attitude of the place, all added up to a surreal experience.

My sister bunnies—and you will excuse my stating the obvious—were dumb as posts, but they were more than a match for the men who drooled into the place. I think this was when I first realized the astonishing depths of male stupidity.

If I could have been cured of my love of foreigners, it would have happened here, because a large number of club regulars were Asian and European, the most bizarre parade of cretinous imports imaginable. Nothing foreign was human to me back then.

They would slap their flippers together and bark for drinks, and they held their liquor like a group of staunch 10-year-olds experiencing their first taste of a MaiTai. We bunnies had to fight them off with sticks.

This was not what Joanie meant, of course, when she suggested I move back to the city on her terms. Or perhaps it was all too close to her own experience to be comfortable. Billy Rose was nowhere in evidence, but there was a picture of Hugh Hefner hanging in the dressing room.

My mother soon enough sprung me from the rabbit hutch and put me on the runways of the Garment District. Through her connection, I got a job modeling for Gillis McGill's agency. They called us "mannequins," and I suppose I should have been insulted by the term, but for a lot of my co-workers it represented a step up.

"If you're a sex object, use it," Joanie said. Thanks, Mommy, thank you for those pearls of wisdom. I'll do the same for my own daughter, but if you'll excuse me now I have to go get my tubes tied.

So I got my first taste of the vast, Byzantine world of the Garment District. It was like a medieval guild picked up and plopped down into a 20th-century metropolis. Xenophobic, incestuous, brutally insular, it floated along on yards of wool jersey and worsted. You could hear the faint buzz and honk of Manhattan outside, you knew it was out there, but you might as well have been on Mars.

In the lofts, offices and warehouse buildings along Seventh Avenue south of Times Square, men with body odor and bulging eyes commit as much of the nation's clothing business as is convenient between their bookmaking opportunities.

I had ridden cabs through these very streets before, with not a clue in the world what was going on around and above me.

There were sweatshops where women did piecework for chump-change. There were jobbers who did a rollicking business selling a single kind of snap, or button, or ribbon.

A lot of the men still wore hats. There were always intense conversations going on in low tones down hallways, or shouted phone calls heard from behind closed doors of offices.

"I fuck you!" they would scream, and slam the phone down. "I fuck you" was the Seventh Avenue equivalent of "good-bye."

And there were runways in those buildings, runways in stale-smelling pre-war showrooms hung with ancient curtains, lit by unsoftened fluorescence. How anyone thought we could look good in such surroundings was impossible to guess. But we trotted out there anyway, showing the line, showing thigh, living up to our billing as human dummies.

Even back then, the world of the Garment District was changing. Jobs were hemorrhaging, going south 40 blocks to the sweatshops of Chinatown, or across the border somewhere where labor could be had for 50 cents a day.

But the lusty garmentos proceeded merrily on their way, like swimmers after the plug was pulled in the pool, feeling the underwater pull of their doom, but being too old or too stupid or too busy reading Racing Form to know what to do about it.

Every two months came "Market Week," when buyers arrived from all over the country to feel the fabric and size up the goods. Our version of the cattle call.

In the dressing room beforehand, there was an exhausted sense of getting up for the big game in a season that never ended. They would make the clothes right on your body. If the seamstresses and fitters liked you they wouldn't stick you with pins all that often.

Once Joanie had tossed me into the lion's den, she felt she had done her duty as a mother. I was left to my own devices. She had made it there, so she fully expected me to do the same. I think the truth was that she had only dim memories of the shittiness of the place. She didn't want to think too much about it, because it might cause those memories to return.

The mannequin girls were considered interchangeable parts, like pattern-pieces or sewing needles. When one of us disappeared or broke down, the garmentos merely ordered up some more. We were constantly losing jobs and shifting firms. Sometimes we were traded like ballplayers.

Every audition for a new company was an excruciating opportunity for sleazy rigmarole. They wanted to see your body. "This job is reserved for women who can fill out a dress well."

That was the polite way of putting it. Usually, they were more direct. "Come on, babe, fish 'em out, let's have a look at 'em."

I remember going into the offices of Abe Schrader Sport. The sales manager was straight out of Central Casting. He embodied the whole worn stereotype of the garmento, right down to his cigar and star sapphire ring.

"You want the job, honey?" he said, tilting back in his chair and smiling. I said I did.

"Then why don't you give me a blowjob?"

Well, I could think of any number of reasons why not. He was a fat, disgusting, smelly cow of a human, for one. The whole scene was just too much of a cliché, for another. But I swallowed my pride, along with his soft, oily dink. I needed the work.

After he finished, I straightened myself and tried to retrieve the flown vestiges of my dignity. "When do I start?"

"You don't," he said, already back at his desk, shuffling papers.

"What do you mean? I did what you wanted, didn't I?"

"Yeah," he said.

"So what's the problem?" I asked, trying to keep the desperation out of voice.

"You didn't swallow," he said. I was about to freak out when he held his pudgy hand in the air. "Not only you didn't swallow, but you didn't gargle."

He began to laugh, and I did freak then, screaming at him and calling him a filthy pig, which is exactly what he was.

But that's also what I was, that's what the whole Garment District was made up of, like a big barnyard. It was a vast, rooting sty of filthy pigs, butting each other aside at the trough, grunting and squealing and eating their young. I was lost in it.

Part of the problem was that I liked my new body so much I had decided to keep it. This required constant maintenance, in the form of diet pills. They call them diet pills because soon enough you start making a steady diet of them.

It was no problem getting a legitimate script for amphetamine in the Garment District. Dr. Feel-Goods hovered
around the place like bookies or whores.

Speed kills, but first it makes you feel like God and then it
dismantles your behavioral touchstones. The days were going
by like loaded boxcars.

What did one more blowjob mean in that dizzying, endless succession of weeks, months, years? I hadn't had a cock
that I liked in my mouth for a long time. I hadn't had a cock
that I loved in my mouth since way back in my Grand Army
Plaza days with Andres Serrano.

Who cares? Sign me up with Scarlet O'Horror. Tomorrow
is another day. Maybe I should have gargled.

Until I learned the real name of the man I knew professionally as Ronald, I had no idea who he was.

One reason why New York is called Fun City is the fact that thousands of visiting businessmen stream through it every day, year in and year out. Everyone knows that traveling businessmen are the horniest people on earth. Something about slipping the leash of the old home town sets their libidos a-pumping and their hind legs a-thumping. They're away from their family, their support system, their moral inhibitions.

They come to New York and go into rut.

They do things that they would never do back home. Of course, New York City offers them a lot of opportunities that they don't have back home. How many pre-op transvestite hookers do you think there are in Des Moines? In the meat district of Manhattan, Mr. Modern-Day Willie Loman can take his pick. Whole packs of "chicks with pricks" patrol the sidewalks down there, luring customers unsuspecting and otherwise. Whatever turns on your appetite, it's on New York's menu.

Ronald was the typical visiting businessman. A dark-haired, pasty-faced Middle Eastern gent who could have been a body double for Alfred Hitchcock, he came into my life after much hesitation and hemming and hawing over the phone.

He would call, ask me a little about myself, tell me a little about himself, but when I asked him if he wanted to book a session, he would always back off.

I'm used to this kind of elaborate telephone chess game. Usually, I don't put up with any bullshit. I cut callers off if they get too breathy or weird or pushy. But I allowed Ronald to call back several times. I had a feeling about him. I felt he needed to work up his nerve, so I cut him a little more slack than usual.

When he finally did walk into my place, I could tell he was immensely pleased with me. Once again, I found myself playing the role of an answer to a man's ultimate fantasy. I am—let's face it—the spitting image of a big-boned Nazi she-devil. I towered over this stooped, elderly gent like doom or madness.

"Are you German, may I ask?" was the first question out of his mouth. Yes, he could ask, and yes, I was part German. My father fled the Nazis just before World War II, I told him. This seemed to cheer him greatly. Fantasy or not, at least we were on the same side. Hitler was supposed to be part Jewish, after all.

Ronald was like a lot of men who hesitated before coming in for a session. Once they actually arrived, there was no stopping them. Within the first few minutes, he told me what he had in mind, and we were off to the dry cleaners.

He had several disgusting personal tics. He was not the cleanest man in the world. His fingernails were grubby and his fingers were stained with ink. It was a wonder he could see at all, since his coke-bottle glasses were always smeared with a thin film of dried sweat.

He dressed beautifully, however. Savile Row suits, exquisite shirts from Hilditch & Key in London. In the winter he came to me wearing an elaborate Russian-style fur hat.

"Sable, from Siberia," he said proudly when I asked the provenance of the fur.

His clothes should have been a tip off that he was more than the secretary/drudge I took him for.

Ronald had an elaborate masochistic scenario worked out for himself, and I was, of course, to play a major role. He was a bad little boy, an aristocratic little boy, with a French nurse ("Miss Lash") who took care of him. This nurse had faithfully kept track of Ronald's numerous misdeeds, and had of late no choice but to refer him to me, "Governess Sonya," for punishment.

In a word, Ronald wanted spanking. Elaborate formulas of verbal abuse were very important to him. These formulas he explained to me in patient, strenuously accented but flawless English.

"When you are punishing me, I want you to say, 'I'm really going to spank your naughty naked buttocks.' Say it."

"I'm really going to spank your naughty naked buttocks," I said dutifully.

"A little more accent on the penultimate word," he requested. I didn't know what "penultimate" meant. Like a lot of people, I thought it meant "beyond the ultimate," which is stupid, because there is no such thing.

But it really means "second to last," and that's something I learned that day from Ronald. You see, if you hang around with intelligent people, some of it is bound to rub off on you.

"Naughty, *naked* buttocks," I practiced, as I helped Ronald off with his clothes.

This process took forever. He was a teetering, tottering wreck of an old man, and I wondered (not for the last time) what the hell I would do if he or one of my other clients ever keeled over during a session. I figured I had two choices. I could dial 911 or immediately clear out of my apartment. I knew of a nice beach in Costa Rica....

Ronald stepped slowly out of his trousers, folded them carefully along the crease, then attacked his hose. Everything of the finest cloth and most conservative cut, I noticed approvingly.

His body was in bad shape. Folds of flesh hung from his body not exactly like Christmas tree ornaments. If the Pillsbury Doughboy ever ages into an octogenarian, I have the perfect model for him.

"If you'll sit and— and— and allow me..." he said, indicating my leather couch. I sat down on it. He settled cautiously across my garter-belted thighs. If he gets any older, I thought, I'm going to need a hoist.

Ronald would fondle my calves and legs while I spanked him. I repeated the formula, reciting his various and sundry wrongdoing for the week, culminating with the magic phrase.

"I'm really going to spank your naughty naked buttocks."

I must have gotten the emphasis right, because the words sent a shiver of pleasure through his body.

Again. "I'm going to spank your NAUGHT-y NAK-ed buttocks!"

This time I meant it. THWACK!

I brought my hand down resoundingly on his doughboy butt. There was blood in the old cheeks yet, since the slap left a bright red welt in the shape of my hand.

Again. "I'm going to spank your NAUGHT-y NAK-ed buttocks!"

Again. Again. I found myself stressing odd syllables, just to keep it interesting. "I'm go-ING to SPANK your naught-TEA, nak-ED but-TOCKS!"

I would shake his bowl-full-of-jelly booty-cheeks to prepare them for the slap. We began to fall into an easy, effective rhythm, Ronald's ass and I. Say the line, shake the flesh, slap! Say the line, shake the flesh, slap! Too bad Ed Sullivan was off the air, I thought, we could have taken our act to the public.

The unvarying tenor of Ronald's fantasies is something that I find characteristic of the men I work with. The human male seems to have all the sexual imagination of a stuck record (a reference that dates me, I know—should I have said a skipped CD?).

Fetishists as a rule are locked into an endless loop of repet-itive erotic drudgery, as if they were mules tied to a mill wheel. The fetishist's partner may be changed, and in this aspect only he craves novelty. The actual fantasy itself is repeated endlessly, like some nightmarish Greek myth.

Ronald really did resemble Sisyphus pushing the poor penile boulder of his libido up a hill, only to have it roll back down again. I wanted to grab him by the lapels and shout at him, "Doesn't it get old? Let's do something different for a change!"

Dear Miss Lash, Ronald has had a very naughty week...

But like Oscar, Ronald was one of those rare men who was nice to be around even after he achieved climax. He was gregarious and friendly, even to the point of inquiring if I knew any of my neighbors in the building across the way. He told me he was in the diplomatic corps, which made sense, since I can practically see the United Nations from my apart-ment, and have dealt professionally with a small but steady percentage of its staffers.

After that first successful session, Ronald became a reg-ular. He often brought me little gifts. As I said, I had not a clue as to his real identity. His face was that of the ultimate everyman—a Semitic, Jewish or Arabic everyman, but an everyman at that. You pass them by the hundreds in New York just going out to get a paper in the morning. Ronald blended in with the crowd.

Then two things happened almost at the same time that led me to deduce Ronald's true name and stature in life, a knowledge that made me fear for my safety (however irrationally) and wish fervently for my former state of blissful ignorance.

I saw a bleary front-page photograph in the New York Times, purporting to show the representatives of a diplomatic team. There was Ronald, front and center.

At least, the man in the photo resembled Ronald. He wasn't stooping, but standing tall, and that made me suspect my eyes were playing tricks on me. Plus the Times photo quality is famously poor, so what I was looking at could have really been a potted plant, for all I knew.

I checked the caption to the photo, and then I knew I was mistaken, for it identified the man I thought was Ronald as a well-known world leader, the former minister of a major Middle Eastern country, a name that even I—who did not follow foreign affairs all that much—had heard once or twice before.

Even then, I didn't want to believe. I chalked it all up to coincidence.

But then later that week I happened to unpack a gift of perfume that Ronald had given me. He had presented it in the bag, Yves St. Laurent's Opium, my sentimental favorite, and I had carelessly tossed it still wrapped into my closet and forgotten about it.

I don't know what caused me to take it out. I wasn't about to clean out my closet. I didn't even need perfume. But when I took the bottle out of the bag his charge slip fluttered to the ground like a blackmail note.

There it was. The same name, the same international player in one of the major political arenas on the globe. My mouth got a little dry and I had to sit down. I wanted to laugh and cry at the same time.

I thought about the implications of this for Middle East peace. Like I said, I don't follow the news all that much. But I knew the fact that a man who controlled the destiny of millions was actually a closet submissive had enormous implications.

Maybe that's what held things up all those years. Maybe the other side hadn't promised to spank his naughty naked bottom, or hadn't accented the penultimate syllable properly.

Then I thought some more. My mind, which has been fed a steady gruel of John Le Carre and Robert Ludlum, started to summon up images of anti-terrorist squads and crack espionage teams.

Ronald must have been followed to my apartment, I thought. These Middle Eastern spy-vs.-spy fuckers are the best at their jobs of anyone on the globe. They know everything. My apartment was bugged. The door was about to be busted down by well-muscled men in black berets.

That never happened, of course. But I have begun to read the newspaper a bit more avidly now. I know to expect a visit from Ronald whenever the U.N. is in session. I've collected snippets and clippings about his career. I even looked up his listing in *Who's Who*. Quite a long, impressive write-up, as a matter of fact.

If they ever think to ask me, I have a sure-fire way to break up any logjams that may occur in Middle Eastern diplomatic negotiations. Simply have a member of the American delegation rise and intone the sacred words.

"I'm really going to spank your naughty naked bottom!"

Look for a red, embarrassed face in the crowd. When you see it, you know you'll have gained useful political leverage, and you can push that advantage on to victory.

Don't thank me. I'd do anything for world peace.

To Governess Sonya

The spanking you gave to Ronald and especially the long lecture you gave him as his naked bottom lay across your knees has had a good effect.
But his conduct is still not sufficiently improved to stop this treatment.
I suggest we proceed with these weekly spankings until he no longer acts like a naughty schoolboy.

Miss Lash

S peed was my life.

According to the old Sixties rule of thumb, you are what you eat. In those days, as the Seventies were about to disco into the sunset, leaving me still marooned in the Garment District, pimping rags for pay, all I ate were diet pills. I had turned into a small, cuticle-sized lozenge, bitter-tasting and hard.

Another tattered piece of Sixties mythology is that drugs take people in order to get high, not the other way around. And it really felt that way, sometimes. I was just a vehicle, a medium, so this substance could achieve the maximum thrill of coursing through my body. The drug was a parasite, feeding off me. I wasn't riding the white tiger. The tiger was riding me.

Speed kills, and death speeds. I was all alone back then, and I was dead.

The odd thing was by that time I was at the top of my form, modeling gorgeous ball gowns at Park Avenue boutiques. They were the kind of lit-up satin fantasies that Anna wore to wow the King of Siam. I would strut around the showroom in these creations like some she-cock, my eyes glittering behind an amphetamine glaze, as tightly wound as an alarm clock wired to a bundle of dynamite.

I think if anyone had crept up behind me and said "boo!," my head would have exploded like a cartoon character's.

And that damned Dylan line kept running through my head. *With your amphetamine and your pearls...* Just like a woman.

Oh, it's such a tired old story by now, the creaky roller coaster you get on when you use speed to get up in the morning and Valiums to go to bed at night. But when you're on the ride, it doesn't matter that Judy Garland rode it before you. The track seems endless. Mommy, Mommy.

She wasn't there any more to answer. She and Fred both died a couple of years apart. Until the end we maintained the illusion that my life was fine, that I had gotten back on my feet after Costa Rica and I was doing work I enjoyed.

But I think in her heart of hearts Joanie remembered what a jungle the Garment District was, how they lunched on your heart down there as casually as on lean pastrami.

She remembered, but she was powerless to do anything about it. I'm sure if she had a million bucks, she would have given it to free me from Seventh Avenue servitude.

The horror, the horror. My mother's last words. Or perhaps she was just calling me a whore.

Not really. I'm just overdramatizing. No one ever thought to tell me Joanie's last words. Perhaps they were too banal to be recorded—not banal/profound, like Voltaire's "More light!" but just plain old Coxsackie boring.

I wish we had a lot more of a good-bye. Not that I would have tried to change anything. Just an exchange of best wishes. Good luck, Joanie. You too, baby.

And of course I'm overdramatizing the Garment District, too. It wasn't all horrible.

I was going out back then with a big-time bookmaker with the Runyonesque moniker of Jake the Rake. In fact, everything about him was Runyonesque: his clothes, which were the epitome of gangster chic, and his accent, which was Bronx all the way. He even mentioned that he had once met Damon Runyon.

"A newspaper guy, so he was full of shit, but he knew his horses." The highest compliment possible in Jake's world, and it escaped from his lips only grudgingly.

"Escaped" is the right word, because he talked out of the side of his mouth, gangster-style, and every mutter came out a little toughened from the battle of getting through. He was 5-foot-2, eyes not of blue but a mean shade of black-flecked brown. Sired by John Garfield out of Jimmy Cagney.

He used to hang out at Lou Siegel's, where the Garment District heavies would come down and kiss his ring and place bets. He had vague connections to the Jewish arm of the mafia. At least, he kept them vague to me, and believe me, I didn't press him on it. He mentioned once that he had a brother who worked for Murder, Inc. (Of course, he didn't say

"Murder, Inc."—he said "Lepke's people.") That was enough for me.

A certain style of short man has always been attracted to me. The compensators, the bantamweights, the big men trapped in small bodies. I become the external metaphor for their idea of themselves. They can say to themselves, I may be the runt of the litter, but here I got this big beautiful blonde on my arm.

If I wasn't enough, Jake was the kind of guy who carried a $20,000 roll of bills stuck into his sock. To him, that was the equivalent of packing a piece, which as Freud will tell you is the equivalent of having a big prick. Jake only wished he could stuff his dick in his sock.

I was sort of distantly amused by the life Jake offered me. He had a lot of people in his thrall, people who would walk up to him with their hats in their hands. Men who were bosses of million-dollar corporations would turn into blubbering jellyfish in front of Jake the Rake.

Bookmakers are a lot of times baby Hitlers, and Jake had some of that in him. He'd let a deadbeat stand there in front of his table at Lou Siegel's, sweating, stuttering, twisting in the wind and pleading for an extension of a gaming debt.

I wouldn't say I learned much from Jake's business methods, but I would be lying if I didn't admit that some of the things I do to my slaves today I picked up watching him at work. One thing I noticed was that those he was cruelest to were the ones first to come back for more.

Jake's life represented a sort of alternative reality to what was going on in the rest of the world. Current events didn't

exist in Jake's life. Newspapers meant nothing to him outside
of the sports pages. The government didn't intrude upon his
existence apart from the time it took him to fix a parking
ticket, which was about six seconds flat.

It makes me laugh, looking back on it and knowing that
Jake's world has pretty much always existed, still exists today, and
probably always will. If you would judge from the magazines,
Vanity Fair, say, you wouldn't even know it was there. It doesn't
follow trends or fashion. It is immune to outside influence.

What it revolves around, mostly, is gambling. Like
fetishists, the denizens of this world never get tired of repeti-
tion. Another horse race, another boxing match, it's always
fresh and new to them. All the kitsch trappings can't mask the
heavy flavor of obsessiveness that comes with the turf.

Garment District gamblers were the only people Jake
hung out with. We'd fly to Las Vegas for the fights. I had a
run of numbers at the crap table once when I was throwing
dice for him, and won $30,000. He gave me $3,000 of it. I
suppose if he were Mr. Nice Guy he'd have given me more.
But generosity wasn't Jake's style. Still, he paid my rent and
living expenses for two years.

On these trips, all the garmentos who came along had
models on their arms, and all the ladies were jacked up on
diet pills the same as I was. It made for some very bitchy
plane rides home. The babes were so cranked that I'm amazed
we didn't achieve some critical mass of amphetamine psy-
chosis. Any little annoyance could have sent us over the edge.
We could have gone berserk and sliced off everyone's pinky
fingers, rings and all.

One afternoon Jake took me into a huge old savings bank on the Upper West Side. The interior reminded me of something out of Dickens, all musty and ancient. There was no one there. I had never seen a bank more bereft of customers. Jesus, I thought, the accounts in this place are probably still written out longhand.

Jake led me into the vault. He had a look on his face like a spider checking his web. He got a safe deposit box from a ghostly bank manager who called him "Mister Jake."

The box was of the large, bigger-than-a-breadbox variety, and it was full of cash. Old, used money, not the new cash machine-style money you see a lot now. These were bills that had been twisted by too many sweaty palms in front of too many three-dollar windows at the track. They had the stink of human despair on them.

Jake gestured to the box. "I've got these all over town," he said, hunching over his horde. "You want one?"

I knew him well enough by that time to know that taking the gift would cost me more in the long run than it was worth, so I refused.

But I was tempted. I actually got physically aroused, looking at all that money in that stuffy little vault on the Upper West Side of Manhattan.

That's what I want, I thought. I want enough money that I have to go visit it like it was a sick relative. I want to send my money flowers and get well cards.

In relations between myself and the world-at-large, I had already determined that I was going to sell out. Now I was just quibbling over the price.

I found out who "Ronald" was through a credit card slip and a front-page photo. Another of my clients revealed himself to me through the medium of television.

I was in the kitchen of my apartment, innocently fixing myself a late-night snack, when I heard a high, wheedling, feminine voice emanate from the box. I had been watching something on public television, and inadvertently left the set on. Charlie Rose, the PBS talk show host, had just introduced a guest.

I stood stock still. I know that voice, I told myself, and raced into the living room.

Sure enough, it was my diaper baby, my two o'clock visitor, the very man who had been transformed into a squalling infant countless times in the very room where I was standing.

Naturally, he looked more austere and dignified in a three-piece suit and a bowtie than he did with his bottom swathed in a white cotton nappy.

He was rumbling and pontificating about the dissolution of the Eastern bloc, and I almost laughed out loud at the contrast. It didn't seem like it could possibly be the same man, but it was. I knew because even on television, the shadow of the Look played behind his eyes.

Let's call him P.M., because he always visited me in the afternoon, invariably scheduling his appointment at two o'clock. This was the slowest time of day for me—between the lunch hour quickies and the after-work rush—and I almost always had time for him.

I had missed Charlie Rose's introduction, so I still didn't know who he was. The host asked his guest about a wide variety of topics. Who would be worthy of such interest? Who could be considered an expert on such varied subjects as Yugoslavia and Michael Jackson?

Whoever he was, P.M. was an expert talker. Words were obviously his metier. He spoke smoothly and forcefully, with supreme confidence that his views were worthy of attention. Here was a guy accustomed to wielding the club of power.

But I knew a different P.M.

Infantilism is the most stripped down and unadorned sub-fetish that falls under the larger rubric of female dominance. Most of the time it is literally stripped down. The infantilists who come to me want to be put in diapers and babied.

I'm not a shrink, so I won't pretend to analyze the motivation of these men. But it's clear that at some stage in their development, something short-circuited deep within their ids, and they formed some sort of association between sexuality and infancy—or, to be more accurate, sexuality and infantilism.

An adult baby, they are called in the biz. An adult male in baby diapers, sucking on the bottle. The immediate reaction is to howl with derisive laughter, of course. What could be more ridiculous? It violates all the norms. Close behind the laughter comes the disgust.

There is something deeply disturbing about a male in diapers—as compared, I suppose, with a diapered female. He is not only ridiculous (as a woman would be, too), he is also shameful, because he has given up that hard-won but natural quality of "being a man." In the battle for maturity, that diaper is his white flag of surrender. And because culture has always relied on mature males to keep it going, to get out there and bring home the bacon, such a figure is instinctively rejected.

More than any other kind of client, I've had people react with more disgust and ridicule toward my infantilists. Boot-lickers, whipping boys, even enema addicts—none of them elicits quite that same response as a wailing 220-pound man wrapped in a diaper.

P.M.'s routine was fairly run-of-the-mill, as far as infantilists go. It was as unvarying as Ronald's and—after two or three sessions—just as brain-numbingly boring to me. He would come wheeling in at precisely two o'clock, expansive and officious. He was still the powerful adult male, capable and confident.

Little by little, though, his manner would become transformed. It's like the infant in him would be awakened by his surroundings. His normally curt and forceful vocabulary would fall away, yielding to coos and mewlings. As he undressed, he would speak in babytalk to himself.

"Na-na wee-wee," P.M. would say.

He always insisted on a cloth diaper. These are very hard to find in adult sizes. The market has moved on to Depend and products like those advertised almost exclusively, for some reason, on the nightly national news. As if watching Dan Rather makes people incontinent.

But all the infantilists I see (and I currently have three or four among my clientele), demand cloth. No disposables for them, thank you very much. They refer back fondly to the swaddlings of their youth. I suppose as a new crop of infantilists come up, they will demand the disposable kind, the diapers of the new world order.

But for the time being, and for P.M., cloth it is. I pin it around him and give him his bottle—one reserved just for him, as he insists. (It would be an awful irony, wouldn't it, to get AIDS from sharing a bottle?) Then he cuddles on my lap and once again it's off—off, I say!—to the dry cleaners.

Throughout this whole process I am quizzing him on his toilet habits of the day, and he is answering me in babytalk. When he is couched in my lap he continues to prattle, and this leads to one of the unfortunate side-products of our client-mistress relationship, for P.M. has truly paint-peeling halitosis.

I've had a couple of hungover afternoons where I canceled our appointment, just because I was afraid I would throw up all over him just smelling it. The Buddha was supposed to have honey-sweet breath, like a child's, even into his old age. Breath like P.M.'s bespeaks a deeper rot of the inner man, a putrefaction of the soul.

And there he was on Charlie Rose, talking up a gaseous storm. Who was he?

When the caption finally came up, I was amazed. The name was instantly recognizable. He was a big man in New York publishing circles, a leading light on the society circuit. Once again, as with Ronald, I had been playing host to a mover and shaker without ever knowing it.

When the implications of it had sunk in, I had to laugh. I have since talked to a friend who once worked under this man, and he described P.M. as an absolute tyrant. Firing people, screaming at them, making secretaries cry. A real pillar of the community, just like Dr. Irving Pie-Hole. But a shit all the same.

Was it too black-and-white to say that these men get out all their urges toward submission in a weekly session with me, then go on to terrorize their friends and associates? Was I unleashing a horde of monsters?

In fact, I had an occasion to find out for myself what P.M. was like once he was out of his diaper. Against all odds, and against all expectation, I ran into him once at a party, totally outside of the private world he and I inhabitated on a weekly basis.

This is, of course, every john's nightmare. To be at their daughter's wedding reception, say, or a social gathering, and suddenly find themselves face to face with the women who balled their jack the night before. It is not only an embarrassing and dangerous situation, it is a violation of a borderline that is designed to be impregnable. Whore and hearth are separate entities for most men, and I've come to believe that it is only such total segregation which allows both of them to exist.

My encounter with P.M. demonstrated this truth anew. It was at a Manhattan book party, affairs which have taken on increasingly desperate airs of late, given the dwindling number of people who actually read. At this one, for a famous writer from the Fifties who was gifting the world with his memoirs, literacy seemed less important than the ability to gobble large amounts of free food while talking volubly at high speed.

"I'd like to introduce you to someone," a friend of mine said, and I turned around and suddenly there he was. P.M., swaddled not in white cotton but in businessman's worsted.

"I know you," he said, his hand coming up automatically to shake mine. You could see his mind work feverishly to place my face.

"And I know you," I said.

Suddenly, it all clicked. P.M.'s hand froze in mid-air. He had been caught off guard. His eyes were like a couple of small balloons that were about to be pricked by a pair of extremely sharp needles. P.M.'s famous verbal facility failed him. He was like a computer that had been given too large a task, unable to do anything else until he finished computing how our meeting might change his life.

When worlds collide. His wife was there. I got a quick flash of me sitting with the two of them in their breakfast nook in New Canaan or Westchester or somewhere, watching the birds come to the feeder in the morning and waiting for the toast to pop. Or her, sitting in the straightback chair in my apartment, watching P.M. and me perform our stylized ablutions.

It would never happen, of course. The two worlds exist only in apartness. Bring them together, they reach critical mass and implode. Even before P.M. turned away, back-peddling like a basketball player guarding an on-rushing steam engine, I knew something irrevocable had happened. I had become a different creature. I was a fairy tale character who had committed the unspeakable crime of stepping out of the book.

I watched him recede into the crowd of party freeloaders. He scooped up his wife and headed for the door. He didn't look back. Maybe he was afraid he'd turn into a pillar of salt.

I never saw him again.

MARCH 14th, 1993

DEAR MISTRESS SONYA:

PLEASE FORGIVE ME, BUT I MUST COME TO SERVE YOU AS I JUST SEPARATED FROM MY ENGLISH VIFE {sic} WHO WAS ALSO A SUPREME MISTRESS.

MISTRESS, NOW TWO MONTHS I HAVE NOT BEEN PUNISH, AND I CANNOT FUNC-TION LIKE THIS, I COULD GO TO A HOUSE OF DOMINATION BUT IT IS NOT THE SAME AS A MISTRESS WHO SOON IS SHE SEE HER SLAVE KNOW WHAT TO DO. ROYAL HIGH-NESS, I ALSO NEED FOUR OR FIVE HOUR SESSIONS AS IN ONE HOUR YOU COULD NOT DO WHAT YOU WANT WITH MY BODY, WHICH I WILL PAY VERY WELL.

NOTHING SURPRISE ME MISTRESS AS I HAVE BEEN A SLAVE SINCE I WAS 14 YEARS OLD, AND THIS IS THE ONLY LIFE I KNOW. I AM EUROPEAN BORN IN BUDAPEST HUN-GARY IT IS WHERE I LEARN THE ART OF PLEASING A MISTRESS. MISTRESS, AS SOON IS I RECEIVE YOUR ANSWER I HUMBLY BEG OF YOU TO ANSWER MY NEEDS, SO WHEN I

COME I DO NOT HAVE TO TELL YOU ABOUT THE SESSION. THANK YOU.

SOON IS I COME TO YOUR APARTMENT, SLAP MY FACE HARD, ORDER ME ON MY KNEES TO LICK YOUR HIGH HEELS AND DEMAND YOUR MONEY, AFTER YOU COUNT THE MONEY YOU SLAP ME IN MY FACE AGAIN AND TELL ME NEXT TIME I HAVE TO BRING MORE MONEY. THEN YOU ORDER ME TO GET NAKED, MAKE ME WORSHIP YOUR FEET AND ORDER ME TO PAINT YOUR TOENAILS.

AFTER I FINISH, YOU FORCE ME TO WORSHIP EVERY INCH OF YOUR BODY, BUT AFTER I FINISH LICKING AND SUCKING YOU, YOU TELL ME, "STUPID SLAVE YOU DO NOT KNOW HOW TO PLEASE A SUPREME MISTRESS FOR THIS REASON I MUST PUNISH YOUR WORTHLESS COCK." I RESPECTFULLY REQUEST TO PLEASE TIE MY COCK THEN PIERCE IT IN THE PIERCING PUT HEAVY WEIGHTS, THEN BURN IT WITH CIGARETTE OR CIGAR, BEAT IT WITH YOUR RIDING CROP, USE YOUR BULL WHIP ON ME, ETC., THEN YOU ORDER ME AGAIN TO TRY TO DO A GOOD

JOB LICKING AND SUCKING YOU, AGAIN I DO NOT DO RIGHT AGAIN YOU PUNISH ME.

ALSO I WISH YOU WOULD RIDE ME AS IT GIVE ME GREAT PLEASURE TO BE YOUR HORSE. AS A GOOD SLAVE I ALSO BE YOUR TOTAL TOILET SLAVE, THIS INCLUDE GOLDEN AND BROWN SHOWERS. MISTRESS, EVERY TIME I COME TO SEE YOU IT BE THE SAME AND I PAY MY TRIBUTE VERY WELL, ALSO GIFTS WHAT EVER YOU WANT I OWN MY OWN COMPANY.

THANK YOU, PLEASE ANSWER SOON IS YOU CAN, SO WE CAN HAVE A LONG FRIENDSHIP AS A SLAVE AND MISTRESS.

SLAVE S.

I had not a monkey but a gorilla on my back, I was running with a midget Jewish bookie, and I had a dead-end job in a high-style fashion ghetto. My only recourse was to do what any normal girl does when she finds she has painted herself into a corner.

I got married.

I don't suppose a weakness for foreigners is a moral flaw sufficient to hurl me into hell or anything, but it has betrayed my life at every step of the way. I've always thought of myself as a fairly sophisticated woman, but how sophisticated can I be when I'm a sucker for an easy accent?

What can I tell you? Accents get me hot.

His name was Michael. He was an architect, University of London educated, originally from South Africa. I wish I could tell you he had left his country in protest over apartheid, but this was not the case. He had left it because he saw the way things were going, and realized that people like him (meaning educated Caucasians) had a very limited future there.

I met him at a cocktail party to celebrate the—what else?—new spring line. I've forgotten why I showed up. The party was thrown by a manufacturer of panties, swimsuits and underwear. Their spring line, it turned out, was almost exactly like their line from last fall. At this level of the business, fashion innovation moves at a glacial pace.

But there were several luscious models wandering around the party in their skivvies, and this had attracted hordes of garmentos. Once they got their drinks and eyed the mannequins, they decided they were bored and the conversation turned inevitably to horse racing.

It was slightly disconcerting, though, to see a salesman seize a model and point proudly to a satin ribbon plastered across her crotch, exclaiming that this frill was what would make this line of panties different from all other lines of panties in the history of creation.

I was immediately attracted to Michael because I knew right away he had nothing whatsoever to do with the garment business. This was because he was actually ogling the mannequins instead of talking about trifectas.

I realized later he was staring at them for an entirely different reason than an ordinary red-blooded male stares at women. But at the time I just thought he was a charmer who looked vaguely like Jean Michael St. Vincent.

"Like the new line?" I asked him, my eyes tight with speed.

'Huh? Oh, yes," he stumbled. "I mean, I don't know. I'm not in haberdashery."

To some ears, the South African accent is thick and demotic. But I had been fed a steady diet of Garment District chat, which is to the Queen's English what the Bronx cheer is to a standing ovation. Michael sounded positively cultured. He had been a mercenary who fought in what was then the Belgian Congo.

"You have a nice body," I said. "Do you work out?" I've always considered the direct approach the best.

Michael seemed to have trouble with his drink, and began to cough explosively. Stand back, stand back, the man has swallowed his nose. Was I overpowering him?

"Rugby," he managed, recovering his voice. "I used to play on a team called the Springbucks in South Africa."

For all its macho posturing, rugby had always struck me as a sport for barely latent homosexuals. All those sweaty bodies rubbing up against each other. On the distaff side, it is the choice sport of lesbians, after all.

I should have listened to my inner voice back then, but the man standing before was so fresh, so attractive, so virile. I couldn't think my way past my first impression. Which was that I wanted to jump his bones.

So we consummated. I never told my new South African boyfriend that I was coming off a torrid affair with a huge strapping black man. Gene would have probably said, "It figures," about my relationship with Michael, saying it proved I was a closet racist all along.

For his part, Michael had a simmering, deep-running sus-picion of all races not his own, which only became clear after I had known him a long time. He was a covert, not overt bigot. I think it comes from drinking the water down there, the racial attitudes are so reflexive and immune to change.

After two years of dating, we got married in New York City. The ostensible reason was so that he could obtain a green card and we could travel together in and out of the country.

Ladies, if you're out there, here is some valuable advice: Never, ever become part of a green card wedding. The mar-riages never work out.

Even Michael's mother, via crackling long-distanced tele-phone conversation from the old country, told me not to marry him. His family was old, stodgy, probably corrupt in ways I could not even imagine. Their fortune was founded on sugar-cane syrup, which they sold to food processors and live-stock feed companies as well as to American producers of chewing gum and candy.

But against Mom's advice we married anyway, and Michael whisked me away to glamorous Toronto for our hon-eymoon, and to make a new life.

In Canada, I couldn't get a prescription refill for my amphetamines. By the second day, I was going slowly bonkers in withdrawal. With increasing desperation, I took taxicab after taxicab, racing around town trying to hit upon a doctor with the proper level of corruption.

Finally, crashing badly, the world turning into a lethal horror in front of my eyes, I demanded that a cab driver take me back to the States. Fuck Michael. Fuck my new husband. I had to fix or I was going to die.

The driver said of course he would drive me back to the border, but politely inquired whether he could see the money first.

"Fuck you, bastard creamhole motherfucker!" I screamed, and I jumped out of the car in the middle of traffic.

The horror, the horror. The world was slamming its derby down around my ears. I didn't actually hallucinate, I just felt so bad, so bad. My life had turned to poison. You're tearing me apart!

I made it back to the 10th floor in the steel and glass apartment building where we were staying. Our bridal suite. I took one look around and immediately attempted to jump out the window. The glass shattered, but the actual frame for the panes was metal, and it held.

Within an hour, I received my final wedding present: Michael had me committed to a psychiatric hospital to come down off the speed. His was probably one of the most honest responses to a wedding ceremony ever recorded. Get hitched and then *immediately commit your spouse to a mental institution.* It's a wonder more people don't react that way to marriage.

The psycho ward was white and cold, like the countryside outside its barred window. For the first few days, I was often under the impression that I had already died, and this was my place for eternity. After two weeks, the worst symptoms of withdrawal dissipated, and the doctors allowed me to return to Michael.

It took me a full three months for the speed heebies to clear from my brain. I was fat, friendless, marooned in

Toronto. Even today, I'm not all that sure I wasn't permanently marked by my charming husband's approach to drug
withdrawal.

Meanwhile, upon my return to our apartment, I discovered that sweet Michael was on a downward spiral of his own.
I realized how serious it was when he pranced into the living
room clad only in pantyhose. Mine.

That was the real secret of his attraction to those Garment
Center models, the day I met him. He wasn't saying "Nice ass,
nice tits," along with the rest of the horny voyeurs there. He
was saying, "Nice silk!"

We began to divide our time between Toronto and
Holland. We owned a car in Europe, and did a lot of touring
on weekends. Paris, Luxembourg and Germany. We always
bought a case or two of wine, which Michael stashed in the
trunk, smuggler-style. It was stuff we could pick up real cheap.
The realization slowly dawned on me that the cheap wine, not
the scenery, was the reason for all the touring we did.

What he needed all this wine for, it turned out, was
enemas. Michael did not stop at cross-dressing. His sexuality
continued to open itself to me like a perverse flower, and it
turned out what he enjoyed most of all was wine enemas.

He told me he liked the way the wine burned his guts and
asshole. He was a master at retaining most of it until the
alcohol was absorbed by his intestines. The wine was nothing
too fancy, just a vin de table or an unclassed Bordeaux. The
procedure made him tipsy as well as tumescent.

The thrill, needless to say, was gone, and I was stuck with
him. Stuck under the lowering, sheep-gray skies of Northern
Europe.

Dear Sonya,

I humbly beg your divine help, most supreme Mistress.

I live in a small town in Mississippi, the kind of place where everyone knows everything about everyone else. I have, of course, told no one about my intense need to be dominated by a Goddess such as yourself. There is no way I can get anyone to understand my need other than you, Mistress.

I feel so lonely and lost here, even though it is my home town. No one knows the real me! I will die if I do not hear from you. I go through my days like I was walking in my sleep.

I must have you to worship, Goddess, to bow down before, to serve. I hunger to place my hot lips against the cool leather of your savage heel. I long to feel your disdain, for I know I am not worthy of you.

Please, Mistress, I most humbly beg of you, answer my prayer. Allow me to be your servant. I prostrate myself before you and await your reply.

Your devoted slave,
Cal

R udolf, king of the night, aging cunthound, disco Hitler, master of manipulation, creator of clubs from Peppermint Lounge to Danceteria to Mars in New York to Tatou in Aspen and Beverly Hills, bisexual bullyboy, Teutonic terror.

Every disco inferno needs its Satan, and Rudolf was ours. He had the type of fame which made Andy Warhol's 15 minutes seem like an excruciatingly long time.

I met him at a club called the Grolier, right around the corner from my apartment. He was a German from his accent down to his manner, his shiny smiling face, his exuberant style. That he was immediately attracted to me proved I was alluring within the tribe as well outside it.

It is probably just a circumstance related to my working in Manhattan, but the majority of my clients are Jewish.

I don't fool myself—I know that one reason I am successful is that I possess queen bitch Nordic looks. Endogamous love, love outside the tribe, is a common characteristic of all peoples.

My Jewish clients love not me but some impossible ideal that I represent. Maybe we should leave it at that, and not draw too many grand conclusions about the reasons why a Jewish man would be attracted to a dominant Nordic woman.

Rudolf proved it worked the other way, too, that as an ultimate Teutonic male he had a jones for me right away. A man like Rudolf, a man whose power and stature is pinned to something as evanescent as the success of his latest club, is extremely hard to take seriously. He's so determined to be in it for the short run.

You wonder what an advanced soul like the Dalai Lama would think of him. What does a rainbow think of the worm that crawls out of the ground after the rain?

But the fact he was attracted to me redeemed him in my eyes. Rudolf, of course, has no difficulty at all taking himself seriously. In his nocturnal world, he is a king. People curry his favor. Brazilian beauties with trust funds. Club kids and soulless Eurotrash. Coke whores and journalists.

After I split with Michael and came back to the States, I felt cored and beaten. I didn't want any kind of world other than the one the clubs of Manhattan offered me, numbing, vacuous, arrogant.

It was actually kind of logical, or it appeared to be in the upside-down world of the Eighties, that clubs and nightlife be elevated to a kind of grand, tragic scale. Studio 54 had earlier propelled this particular brand of decadence into the forefront of the public consciousness.

After that, we were just playing out the dream. People were separated into two camps, one stuck behind the velvet rope and those who had the glamour, money or dope to get past it. The world had broken down into small colonies of the damned. Who were we to argue?

Wallowing in my own self-disgust, I was honored that a king of this world fell for me. The emperor had no clothes, but that made it easier to see he had a big dick. It was the end of the world, and I was in the mood for mindless sex. Rudolf took care of the mindless part, and I supplied the sex.

We had a date that was all foreplay, him groping my ass like Hitler pawing over a map of Poland. The next time I saw him I knew it had to be the real thing. He told me that after that first blue-balled date, he had picked up a hooker and drove her to the front of my building, where she gave him head. Ah, romance.

"I love living in lousy neighborhoods," Rudolf said, as the cab dumped us out in front of a Lower East Side tenement. I trudged up the stairs of his third-floor walk-up. The glamour of his life was really getting to me.

Rudolf's bedroom deserves a place of honor in kitsch heaven. The bed, a grand affair, complete with blood-red sheets, takes up most of the room. The headboard is covered with fake Zebra-skin. Two pair of handcuffs hang down from it like limp dicks.

And mirrors, lots of mirrors, as befits a soul of such supreme self-absorption. A large bowl of condoms, just like at a swing club. A three-foot statue of the Virgin Mary, her arms outstretched. Above all this, to remind Rudolf of his roots, a mirrored ballroom globe.

He was not the finest host. If you want a drink at Rudolf's, you have to ask for it. I learned on subsequent visits that it was not just this night his mind was elsewhere, it was all the time.

His body was smooth and hairless, and since I abhor hairy men, I liked it. That and the fact he was hugely hung.

"Take off your blouse and stockings," he commanded, twisting my skirt above my waist. I slid out of my clothes and into his arms.

"Your body was made for fucking," quoth Rudolf.

He completed the seduction by pivoting me around and bending me over a table. Not just this night but every time I fucked him, Rudolf's sexual technique was to lovemaking what disco was to music. Among other things, loud. When he comes, it is with an animal roar louder than any man I have ever been with.

He came that evening not in the rubber he had slipped on before entering me, but in my face, my hair, my shoulders. After pummeling me with his huge cock, he wanted to finish off with a blowjob, so I had complied. I had to cram him into my mouth to get it all in.

"How does it taste?" Like a dentist, he asks you questions when your mouth is full. Unable to answer, I gamely nodded.

At the last moment, he disengaged from my lips and ejaculated all over me.

In the porn world, the verb for that is "blorch." Rudolf blorched on my face and hair that first night, and it was like the cherry on a mountainous sundae of shit. I liked it. It fit my mood perfectly.

We didn't have much to say to each other after we screwed. I caught a cab on East Houston Street. The cabby was surly and unhappy like I was, and we made a good match as we bumped uptown. The streets were as pocked and treacherous as the Sea of Fertility.

There are times when late night cab rides can be the most exhilarating thing in the world, when you are hitting every light and banging through the greatest city in the world at 50 or 60 miles an hour. Hellhound on your trail.

"No stars tonight," I said.

"Fuck you," my driver said to me in Pakistani. We hit a pothole where all the surviving mayors of New York City could have sat comfortably and played a rubber of bridge.

The sea of futility. My new name for Manhattan.

Later on—much later on—Rudolf would do me the invaluable service of putting me in a frame of mind where becoming a professional dominatrix seemed not only logical but inevitable. Even more than Willie, he was the one man who allowed Susan Shellogg to become Mistress Sonya. That was further on down the line. But this night—the first one I spent with Rudolf—represented that fateful first step that starts off a thousand-mile journey.

The taxi driver glared at me in the rear view. I was just glad he was watching the road, even if it was the road behind us. I stared out the window and carefully picked the dried come of the king of nightlife from my hair.

I never, ever get involved with my clients. This is a fairly easy decision to make, since unlike a straightahead prostitute, I see men who wear their weakness like a badge of honor. They tend to accept their lack of confidence, and actually revel in the fact that they are meek human beings.

I've heard of working girls who fall for johns, and I even have a friend who married one of hers. She was a former call girl (she used to work for Sydney Biddle Barrows, the famous "Mayflower Madam"), a one-time porn star, down on her luck, doing work at a massage parlor.

In walked a socially inept, painfully self-conscious john. He turned out to be an M.D., a psychiatrist no less. The two of them somehow managed to get past the ritualized exchanges of hooker and john and connect as people.

They are married now and have a family. She gets him to prescribe designer drugs for her, and he gets her to bake him chocolate cakes. The wonders of the heart. Or, like my friend used to say: Oh, those humans.

That story is so unlikely it is the exception that proves the rule. The hooker's code of ethics usually requires strict adherence to what in high school the boys used to call the "Three F's": find 'em, fuck 'em and forget 'em.

I've never broken that rule, except once.

Let's call him Skippy, after George Bush's evil twin in "Doonesbury." He was an old money WASP—the kind a friend of mine used to call a "yellowjacket WASP," whether in reference to their dress or their sting, I was never quite sure.

Skippy did, in fact, know George Bush, because he worked at an investment bank in which Bush had an interest. He used to bore me to tears telling me what George said, what George did, what George liked. Although, come to think of it, there is a shade of the Look in George Bush's eyes that always made me think he would make a good client...

Skippy was about 35 when I first met him, a gangly, carrot-headed scion of an old banking family. His grandfather had founded a brokerage firm that is one of the top two or three in the world. There were pictures on the wall of Skippy's apartment, showing his father dating Olivia de Havilland, the family with Eisenhower, everyone vacationing at his grandfather's seashore estate.

The apartment was off Fifth in the 70s and stank delicately of Skippy's old money background. Not only the photos on the wall, either. The furniture was of the slightly shabby variety which was expensive at one time but now was unabashedly threadbare. Skippy affected not to notice. His place was a bachelor pad, and he liked it comfortable. Metropolitan Home not interested, and not invited.

I saw him first as a client. He called me up with a fairly straightahead nurse-patient fantasy—yet another flavor in the jam-packed ice cream case of female domination.

This is such a common one that it makes me think something kinky may be going on in our nation's hospitals. Sponge baths, enemas and rectal thermometers are just too much for some people, I guess, and the exquisite starchiness of a nurse's uniform sends them into Never-Neverlands of joy.

Skippy wanted me to come to him, and when I got to his apartment, I saw why. At first glance it was just an ordinary WASPy sort of place. Skippy himself impressed me with his 6-foot stature, his aw-shucks good looks. The surroundings, as I said, sent their own sort of message, of which the subtext was money-money-money.

But the apartment also held a secret. Skippy had a special room off his bedroom, something like a Batcave of his id.

It was a little cubicle, painted a bland shade of yellow and outfitted like a hospital room. It had the narrow metal bed with the pivoting tray. A tiny television which swung out from the wall on a telescopic arm. An equipment closet with bedpans, stethoscopes and thermometers. Even, as I was to learn, a nurse's call button.

"All expenses paid, dear," Skippy had told me on the phone, so I went down to 14th Street and bought myself a nurse's uniform, as he had instructed. Like the sly bitch I am,

I bought it one size too small (over the saleswoman's objections), so I would look like I was spilling out of it.

Also as per Skippy's instructions, I wore a garter belt underneath the uniform. Mine was of black glove leather, and it framed a g-string thong of the same buttery soft material. My stockings were back-seamed silk. Size tall.

Hmmm, I thought when I checked my look in the mirror before going out. Even I would fuck me.

As we spoke in Skippy's living room he proved to be an affable, garrulous young gent, and I must say I was attracted to him. I liked his sense of irony, his gentle self-deprecation, traits that I think are bred in these people. To the manner born.

"I'll just scoot into the other room, and when you see that light go on over the door, I wish you'd come in and see me," he directed, beginning to tremble a little bit with the excitement of it all.

I idly looked over the family photos and fingered the linen as I waited. The light went on and a small, childish voice yelled out, "Nurse! Nurse!" It was so plaintive that at first I thought Skippy had a little nephew in there with him.

But it was just him, in the coffin-sized bed with the covers pulled up to his chin. He had transformed himself into a 12-year-old boy.

It was the first time I had seen the Batcave, and I was astonished at the verisimilitude. I had stepped into a Star Trek transporter and had been beamed uptown to Mount Sinai or St. Luke's. There were even flowers and a Styrofoam pitcher on the little bedside stand.

I went over and felt the patient's forehead. It was actually hot to the touch, and I jerked my hand away, surprised. I learned later that Skippy had a little heating pad he applied to his forehead in these instances. Everything in service to the truth.

"I think it's time to take your temperature," I said.

He objected, kicking at the covers in a 12-year-old kind of way, but I insisted sternly. I walked to the equipment closet and chose a thermometer from a gleaming cupful of them.

"Turn over," I commanded.

"No-oooo," Skippy wailed.

"Do you want me to call your mother?" I asked, whipping the sheets down. Again, I was astonished at the completeness of the effort: he was wearing a standard-issue hospital gown.

Which made the rear entry required to take his temperature rectally all the easier. Something must have occurred back there in the dim recesses of Skippy's convalescent past, because he got harder than Chinese algebra (as Tom Waits used to say) as soon as I inserted the probe into his anus.

I sat down in a little chair to wait, being careful to expose generous amounts of garter. All this was as I had been directed to do. Skippy squirmed and whimpered in bed, rubbing his crotch against the sheets, peering over to glance up my starched white dress. He climaxed that way, no muss, no fuss, without me having to help him along at all.

He had told me to leave the room after his orgasm, and I did so, discreetly. When he emerged a few minutes later, he was his old hail-fellow self, dressed once again in L.L. Bean khaki pants and black Kenneth Cole topsiders. He was beaming.

"That went very well," he said. "Look, would you like to stay and have a drink or something?"

I would, and I did. It is hard for me to reconstruct what followed exactly, but I wound up spending the whole evening with him, and at the end of it, fucking him in the little hospital bed.

It was the only time I have ever had sex with a client. But his manner was so winning, and his fetish seemed so harmless, that I let my natural inhibitions erode. No money changed hands for that second round of nurse-patient psychodrama.

In fact, I saw him many times after that, playing for free each time. We went out. He began to introduce me to a few of his friends. I think I was actually trying to imagine myself as Mrs. Skippy, fitting cleanly into his old money world like a hand into a glove.

A white latex surgical glove. For this was the only way Skippy could achieve an erection, in the little hospital cubicle off his bedroom. We used to talk about slipping into Beth Israel and reconstructing his fantasy there, but we never did. Although I vamped and rubbed, sucked and bumped, the only way he could get it up was as a regressed 12-year-old tonsillitis patient.

It finally got to me. I was in the middle of saying brightly, "Time for your temperature," for perhaps the fiftieth time. I saw it all stretching out in front of me, an unending series of bedchecks.

Even if I became Mrs. Skippy Third the Third (and it was ludicrous of me to even think he would pop the question), what then? Same old routine. Smear some more Vaseline on the rectal probe, dear.

The flowers on the bedside stand, I had noticed, were artificial. They would remain there, always blooming, never wilting. In 20 years, those flowers would look exactly the same as they do tonight, I thought. It depressed me awfully.

After that evening, although Skippy called me repeatedly to try to schedule a session for pay, I never saw him again.

Dear Susan:

Happy April 15th. It's my least favorite day of the year, even more so this year because my accountant gave me awful news about my taxes.

The following is some general information about health insurance You asked me to obtain for You.

First, i think it's important for You to accept the philosophy that 1) it's vital, even critical, for You to be covered by health insurance (without it You could become a ward of the state if You are incapacitated and if You don't have inherited wealth or access to wealth and 2) it is much more cost-efficient when obtaining health insurance to deal with an independent agent instead of an agency.

i have done some research with several independent agents and found that the plan i have outlined here is the most efficient one for the money. You would need to find an independent agent licensed to handle this insurance (or you could obtain the insurance through the agent i have contacted here).

You also may be interested to know that this plan does not require You to take a physical. However, under the terms outlined, it is assumed that You are in good health, that You are a non-smoker and that You are not alcoholic or a drug user (marijuana does not count as a drug). If You smoke (somehow i don't think You do), the monthly payments are higher.

When You told me You didn't have health insurance, i was amazed, but even more, i was concerned. i'm certain You are aware of this, but You are running a tremendous risk by being uncovered. A relatively simple matter (herniated disc or even gall bladder problems or appendicitis) could cost You up to $10,000. Without trying to sound like a voice of doom, if You were to slip off a curb and break a leg, the cost could be as much as $3,000 and more than $7,500 if surgery were required.

If You wish me to obtain more information on this, please let me know and i will do that for You. i want very much to demonstrate that i respond rapidly to all orders.

Thanks very much for sending Your picture. You looked beautiful in it. If You have other pictures, i would love to receive one.

i also was curious about Your line of questioning to me during our brief phone conversation earlier this week, particularly your questions about my masturbation routine. i believe i mentioned to you in my previous letter that i have been placed on masturbation schedules in the past. In other words, i have been told precisely when i could and when i could not mastur-

bate or do anything else that would bring me any physical pleasure.

Thanks, also, for giving me the honor of obtaining information pertaining to health insurance for You. It is my fondest wish that You let me know what else i can do to please You.

Yours sincerely,
slave donald

There ain't nothing like a dame, unless it's a man dressed like a dame. Of all my clients, those who ask me to force them to dress as women strike me as the most amusing.

The transvestite may be the new man of the Nineties, like the gay man was the man of Eighties. TVs come in all sorts of flavors, from drag queens to pump-wearing truck-drivers with five o'clock shadows under their rouge, to killer pre-ops who can "pass" in the full light of a sunny day. At noon. Under a klieg light.

The best legs I've ever seen in the world (besides my own, of course) led up from the floor and ended, a tall drink of water later, at the slim, prick-equipped, drop-dead body of a beautiful Puerto Rican pre-op. Pre-op, as in "pre-operation," meaning he was taking the hormones that would eventually enable him to switch genders.

Transvestites are different than transsexuals. Transsexuals actually want to be the opposite sex, and they are convinced that they are trapped in the body of wrong gender. Transvestites just get off on dressing like the opposite sex. It is a sensual thrill for them to feel the lace panties, the silk stockings, the tightened corset.

My clients fit into a strange, twilight zone species of the genus transvestite, sub-genus forced cross-dresser. They usually do not cross-dress willingly. The only way it means anything to them, sexually, is if they were forced into it.

They cry, they wail. Oh, please mistress, don't make me do this. Oh, please, please, what if she sees me, what if she sees me. "She" being the mommy-boogie, I suppose.

Oh, for Christ's sake, you want to scream at them. It's only a pair of panties. Put them on and stop blubbering.

A thin, quivering bag of protoplasm named "Jim" was my first cross-dressing client. He came from New England, and was a nuclear engineer at a power plant up there. Shades of Homer Simpson. I was hesitant to accept him as a client at first, not only because I was inexperienced in his particular fetish, but because I was afraid of rogue isotopes rubbing off his skin and giving me an instant cancer or making me glow in the dark.

He was not over-attractive as a man, and no day at the beach as a woman, after I got through with him. I wasn't proud of my creation. In fact, he resembled nothing so much as a mental ward reject, turned out of her bed because she was harmless to the public, forced to wander the streets like a ghost.

Part of this effect was due to the fact that Jim never mastered lipstick. He would always place a large smear around his mouth as if his tongue were the bull's eye and his Revlon scarlet were the outer ring. It gave him a mawkish air, and he didn't need much help with that.

The cross-dressers always show up for their sessions with suitcases, usually little blue Samsonite overnighters from the Fifties. I tell them that I have a large enough wardrobe closet they ought to be able to find something to wear (or be forced to wear). But I soon realized I was missing the point. It was not just any clothes that these men wished to see themselves in. It was a particular frock, a special red dress, a sexually charged pair of mules. The more ridiculous, the better.

Jim was fat, so he liked corsets. "This is a 44," he said that first session, hauling a sail-sized spinnaker out of his suitcase. "I'm hoping to eventually get down to a 36."

Yeah, right, I thought. When shrimps learn to whistle.

The routine was simple. It turned out that Jim simply did not deserve his manhood. He needed to be stripped and whipped and then outfitted in the most ludicrous outfit possible, meaning women's wear.

"Put it on," I said, unfurling the corset like I was a grand marshal at a Flag Day parade.

"I don't want to," he whined.

"I don't care what you want. You are going to put it on. You are too pathetic to prance around in men's clothes. I'm going to dress you up as a dolly. Put it on."

Sigh, whine, tears, the tracks of his mascara. Finally he winched himself into it.

Then I began to lace him up. This process was to Jim what a shampoo bodyrub with Cindy Crawford on a wet air mattress would be to some men. An impossibly sexy turn-on.

With each yank of the laces, Jim's cock got more engorged. It peeked like a punctured eggplant out of the panties I had forced him to wear.

"Tighter, mistress, please," he said. I braced my boot against the small of his back, its heel digging into his back like, well, like a stiletto. I was working up a sweat. I wrapped the laces around my fingers like dental floss and strained backwards. I felt all the air puke out of him with a soft flatulent noise.

Jim couldn't move very well rigged up this way, and I was forced to root through his bag and pull out the dress he wanted me to drag him into. Once again, I meditated on the power of submission. I was the dominatrix, and he was supposed to serve me in all things. But now I was literally his valet.

I suddenly wondered what it would be like if I really dominated this man. Shut up! Stop whining! Take that ridiculous outfit off! Lose some weight! No one cares about your silly perversions. Go away and never bother me again.

Jim really believed in me only as a character in his fantasy. The real way to assert my dominance would be to reject that fantasy altogether. What does a sadist do to a masochist?

"I don't want to, Mistress," Jim was saying. "Please don't make me."

"Oh, it's just a little red dress. Grow up."

He was crouched on his hands and knees in front of me, the corset forcing his body to curl in on itself like a claw. My words made him peer up at me, startled. There was a moment there when he managed to penetrate the fog of his fetish and realize he was in the room with another human being.

"Wah...?" he managed, totally baffled.

For a moment it could have gone either of two ways. I could have sat him down and explained my whole life to him right then and there. Or I could step back into my role and go on with the game. Which I did.

"Maybe you deserve to wear it after all," I said. "Maybe you're a sissy-girl underneath all that body-hair."

Jim smiled loopily and sank beneath the waves of his need.

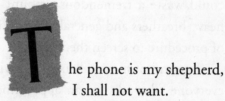

he phone is my shepherd,
I shall not want.

My business depends so much on the phone that I regard it as my lifeline, my security, my other. They are out there, trembling in their need, my clients, and they come to me first through the phone. Sometimes I let them come to me in person, sometimes I stop them after the first few sentences of their call.

The modern telephone has developed into a sort of pseudo sexual organ. Even if the government wanted to stop all this sex business from going on, it couldn't. It would have to tap every phone in America. The telephone frees communication between consenting adults from outside interference. Sexual technology—or technology used in the service of sex— has galloped far ahead of any control that can be placed on it.

I use my telephone not so much to solicit customers—my advertisements do that—as to screen them. My conversation with someone calling me on my business line has a somewhat skewed quality. I ask them what they want, couching the question in perfectly bland language ("What kind of fantasy are you interested in?"). I ask them their ages, what they do for a living, if they are in good health (for some reason, this query always elicits a laugh).

I'm not looking for information. I am checking to see if they are serious, if they really are who they say they are. I could waste a tremendous amount of time on prank calls, heavy breathers and general weirdos, if I didn't have some sort of procedure to screen them out.

I get rid of more callers than I wind up seeing. I don't see everyone who asks for an appointment. I have to know: an appointment for what? If they don't know that much about domination, or if they are unsure about the delineation of their fantasy, then I simply don't see them.

I screen out 90 percent of the novices who call, simply because they require too much time to deal with. Anyone who uses a hushed tone or talks quickly, or has any hint of the insidious in their voice, I reject out of hand. If a caller is graphic on the phone, I hang up. Anyone who says anything remotely sexual with the first few words, I am simply not going to see. Too many people call me looking for free phone sex.

Over the course of thousands of calls, I have gotten to where I can green- or red-light someone after one or two sentences. The sheep and the goats are that easy to separate.

I deal only with callers who are polite and businesslike, and who seem to know what they want. I know that most serious callers—the ones who end up being paying customers—call at certain times of day. There is a wave of serious callers around lunchtime, and another from 4 p.m. to 6. Such are the tides of men's desire—or maybe it's just then that they steal a few minutes from work.

I quote Jimi Hendrix a lot. Are you experienced? It's my most important question. I am looking for people who have been through the jungle of S-M in Manhattan and are searching for something more, something better.

What follows are edited transcriptions of my business calls. All these conversations occurred over the course of a week. Of course, there are many calls I did not include. But those that are here are a representative sample.

Sonya: Hello, how may I help you?
I am inquiring about your ad.
Sonya: Do you have any experience?
No, I don't.
Sonya: You're a novice?
Yes, I am.
Sonya: What type of work do you do?
I'm a corporate attorney.
Sonya: What type of fantasies are you interested in?
Basically, I have a foot and leg fetish.
Sonya: "Basically"? What's basic about it?
I would be very interested in worshipping your feet and legs, which were very beautiful in the photograph.

Sonya: I'm sorry, I don't deal with novices.
[Click]

*   *   *

Sonya: How old are you?
Thirty-nine.
Sonya: What type of work do you do?
I work for a recycler. I drive heavy equipment, front end loaders, tractors, tractor trailers.
Sonya: What type of experience have you had?
I've been to a few mistresses as a submissive, for bondage, discipline, foot worship.
Sonya: You're covering a lot of territory. What is your particular fantasy?
To be tied up and whipped—lightly, not severely.
Sonya: With what?
Small whips, hands, maybe a paddle. My nipples clamped with clothespins.
Sonya: Wooden or plastic?
Wooden.

*   *   *

Sonya: How can I help you?
I'd like to be transformed.
Sonya: Transformed? From what to what?
I'd like to be transformed into a sissy maid.
Sonya: What are you now?
I'm a man who needs to be transformed.

*   *   *

Sonya: How old are you?
Thirty.
Sonya: Where do you work?
I work in a hospital as a lab technician.
Sonya: I really don't think you make enough to afford me.
I can try.
Sonya: Trying isn't good enough. How much do you make in a week?
I make $350.
Sonya: Let me give you some advice: take $50 of that money and invest it in therapy.

*   *   *

I was wondering if you'd be traveling to Chicago anytime soon.
Sonya: If you'd supply a first-class round-trip ticket to Chicago, plus my fee and expenses, I'd be glad to come to Chicago.
[Pause.] *No, I was just wondering if you'd be in Chicago.*
Sonya: You thought I just might happen to be in Chicago and that you could schedule an appointment with me?
Yes.
Sonya: Hardly, sir.
[Click]

*   *   *

Sonya: How old are you?
I'm 38.

Sonya: What kind of work do you do?

I'm a photographer.

Sonya: Are you experienced?

I've been to Ava Taurel a couple times.

Sonya: What did you do there?

I'm interested in teasing. Teasing and discipline. I have a student-teacher fantasy that I haven't asked anybody to do.

Sonya: Why not?

I didn't think they'd get it right.

* * *

I want you to lash my back open.

Sonya: I would seriously suggest that you get psychiatric help immediately.

You are a colossal fool!

[Click]

* * *

I'm pretty much of a novice.

Sonya: Pretty much?

I've had one session.

Sonya: Who with?

Mistress Lea.

Sonya: What do you do?

I'm an accountant.

Sonya: What sort of session did you have in mind.

I'm interested in an interrogation-type fantasy.

* * *

Sonya: How old are you?
Thirty-six.
Sonya: What do you do?
I'm an accountant.

*   *   *

Sonya: How old are you?
Forty-six.
Sonya: What do you do?
I'm an accountant.

*   *   *

Sonya: How old are you?
Thirty.
Sonya: What do you do?
I'm an accountant.

*   *   *

Sonya: How old are you?
Just turned fifty.
Sonya: Congratulations. What type of work do you do?
I'm an accountant.

*   *   *

Sonya: How old are you?
Thirty-eight.
Sonya: What do you do?
I'm an accountant.

*   *   *

Sonya: How old are you?
Twenty-seven.
Sonya: What kind of work are you in?
I'm an accountant.

*   *   *

Sonya: What kind of fantasy are you interested in?
Bondage, domination.
Sonya: Where are you from?
Singapore.
Sonya: Do you have any experience with female domination?
No, this is my first time.
Sonya: What do you do?
I'm a banker.

*   *   *

I'm looking for training.
Sonya: What kind of training?
Feminization.
Sonya: How old are you?
Fifty-one.
Sonya: What do you do for a living?
I'm a pilot.
Sonya: What kind of planes do you fly?
DC-8s.
Sonya: And you're based here?
No, actually I'm just visiting. My wife's on a shoot.

Sonya: A shoot?

She's in advertising. They have a shoot in Central Park. I'm here at a hotel with my wife, so I have to be kind of discreet.

Sonya: Does your wife ever cross-dress you?

No, but she wants me that way.

Sonya: She wants you that way?

I've been laid off for a year, due to the recession in aviation. I've been taking care of the house. She wants me to be feminized. She says that she's making the living, and that I should be the housewife.

Sonya: Why doesn't she dominate you?

She doesn't know how.

Sonya: You want to be turned into a sissy maid?

A housewife.

Sonya: If you have a penis, how can you be a housewife?

She says I can be dressed as one. I could be buttfucked with her dildo.

Sonya: She has a dildo? Why would she want to use it on you?

I guess she's bisexual.

*   *   *

I'm calling for Mistress Sonya.

Sonya: This is she.

Sorry?

Sonya: This is Mistress Sonya.

This is you? Very good.

Sonya: This is a bad connection. Where are you calling from?

I'm calling from Austria, from Vienna. But I would like to come to New York as soon as possible. I travel a lot because I am a flight attendant.

Sonya: Why don't you call me when you get to New York?

Yes, I will, but the first question I have—please give me a real fair, honest answer—I look for extremely hard and a real cruel mistress, and I don't know if you can be that.

Sonya: How cruel?

I'm a real slave. I'm only 27 but I have a lot of experience. The problem is I could not find in America a real tough mistress, the real hard and strict mistress. Why is it so hard to give the hard sessions for the Americans?

Sonya: Maybe you haven't met the right one. I can be very cruel, but I wouldn't call myself tough. Cruelty has nothing to do with toughness.

I don't understand you.

Sonya: Listen, this connection is very bad. Why don't you just call me when you get to New York?

Yes, okay.

[Click]

I had entered the world of S-M blindly, not knowing where it would land me. One day I was a downtown girl haunting the fringes of the club scene. The next day I was a dominatrix. It wasn't like I had any cogent plan.

Experience has always had a way of bucking and jumping beyond me, dragging poor Susan along behind it like a greenhorn with her foot caught in the stirrup.

I think it's that way for a lot of people. Not many of us have the ability to shape our lives. We don't formulate Five Year Plans. Or, like the communists, we may have them, but we conveniently forget to apply them.

S-M has been a wild ride for me. I didn't really realize how wild, how much it was changing my life until I was fairly deep into it. By then it was too late to draw back and ask myself if I really wanted those particular changes to come about. They had already happened.

One change, the most disturbing change to me, was emotional. I woke up one day, months after being in the business of female domination full-time, and realized that some essential pattern in my emotional life had shifted.

My romantic life up until that point had been a fairly consistent one, despite the evidence presented in these pages. I was into what a friend of mine used to call sequential monogamy.

I had a series of boyfriends I was happy with for a while, before they peeled off their masks and revealed themselves to be an assortment of werewolves, zombies and bloodsuckers. The arc of my affairs had always been the same: a small bump of ecstasy followed by a long grim slide into boredom and despair.

Still, it was a life. And it was not that different from the romantic lives of a lot of people I knew. We were all having trouble, there at the end of the millennium, putting together anything resembling an extended, committed relationship. Hell, a lot of us were having trouble putting together a coherent sentence.

In the months after I became a dominatrix, my long parade of boyfriends suddenly came to an end. I experienced my first dry spell since my days in Coxsackie. At first, I thought it was because I was just too overburdened with work. Maybe the men were still calling, I thought, and they were just getting a busy signal.

I didn't want to face up to the truth. I didn't want to admit to myself that the reason I didn't have any boyfriends was that I wasn't pursuing them. I was getting something I needed from my clients.

What I was getting wasn't sexual—not totally, at least. Although that would be the easiest explanation for the shift in my emotional life, it's not the case. I never climaxed during a session with a client, usually never even got aroused.

No, there was something deeper, stranger, more intense going on than mere sex. After all, if I wanted to screw someone, that had always been easy enough. As a general rule of thumb, it's easy to get sex off men. Easier than getting it off women, although it's harder to get *good* sex off men.

But what I was getting from my clients was something else. It was human connection of the most basic kind. I don't want to get too grand here, and make claims for something that isn't there, but I began to realize that I was feeling a bond with the men who came to visit me. Without admitting it, I had allowed myself to feel very close to them. I had entered their world.

It wasn't supposed to happen that way. My dalliance with S-M was going to be a simple monetary transaction. I was the human jukebox, and they were simply plugging me with quarters to hear their favorite song. There couldn't be any emotional danger in something as mechanical as that, could there?

But something went wrong along the way. I first realized it with a slave whose name I don't even remember now—I've probably blocked it out.

I do recall the session precisely. It was an afternoon in fall, after that first summer I hung out my shingle as a dominatrix. I remember because the northern light that comes into my apartment at that time of year is of a particular quality. A snapshot I took of that session—a mental snapshot, that I hold in my mind—is bathed in the silver, washed-out light of autumn.

The slave is there, too, centered in the shot, his face twisted around and looking up at me. He has curly brown hair and large round eyes. He is not particularly good looking, or special in any way that might explain why I've remembered him.

But there was a moment with him that I can't shake. He was a B&D freak—bondage and discipline. Usually I don't trouble with that brand of fetishist. Like I said, my knot-tying skills are not the finest. B&D was just too much trouble for such a limited return.

But this slave, I recall, drifted across the border into B&D terrain in the course of his single session with me. I had tied his hands with the long bullwhip, and a look of pleasure crossed over his face. I knew I was onto something. I began to rig ever more elaborate lariats, hitches and hogties. I felt like a combination of Will Rogers and Isadora Duncan.

Pretty soon he was cinched and winched, tied within an inch of his life. I could have done anything to him. I was behind him, and had brought him to his knees. He looked back at me with those tremendous eyes, and I found myself drowning in them.

Everything stopped for a long moment. I felt seized by the awful extremity of his pleasure, touched by it, and finally broken by it.

It was impossible, but I swear I felt his heart pounding not through his ribcage but from his back. It beat against my thighs as if it were trying to break free from his chest. Everything about him was bonded and tied down, but his heart and eyes were soaring. I felt like taking his head in my hands and tenderly kissing him, Mother Mary style.

Maybe I actually did that. But what I remember was breaking away from him and walking across the room, breathing hard, momentarily confused.

He had fallen in a heap to the floor. It took me a good minute before I was ready to cross back over and release him. The session was over, I told him, curt. He began to complain his hour wasn't up yet. He had no conception of what he had done to me. I refunded half his money and pushed him out the door. I didn't say anything about calling me back after one o'clock the next day, either.

That was it. I had gotten a little too close. I had successfully pinched it off, and it was all over. Or so I thought. His face kept floating up to me later in the day and before I sank into sleep that night. Twisted around, looking up at me. Our eyes meeting. Feeling his heart.

It disturbed me. I took a few days off, went up to Coxsackie, and tried to sort things out. I began to catalog other too-close-for-comfort incidents, too.

What was going on? Was it all getting to me? I prided myself on being the girl who could stand anything, the one with the Timex psyche. Takes a licking and keeps on ticking.

But I had been arrogant. You can't be a feeling human being (did I qualify?), enter into something as explosively personal as S-M, and expect to come out totally unaffected.

The more I thought about it, the more I realized that the barrier I had set up between my professional and personal lives was permeable. A simple example: when I was in good sexual feather, when my sensuality was wide-open and in good working order, I noticed that my sessions with my clients tended to go better.

This makes a certain kind of undeniable sense. When the juices are flowing, you're better at almost anything you do. If you're a typist in the typing pool and you're getting good sex from somewhere (even if it's only from the end of your finger), you're going to hit those keys with a little more precision.

But I resisted that thought vigorously. I didn't want any spillover from my private sexual life to bubble up during a session. I wanted to be Mistress Sonya, the Robot Queen.

Another thing I noticed is that my sexual antennae had become sensitized to all flavors of submission among men. Whereas before, I could recognize the Look only occasionally, now I became attuned to finer, more subtle indications of sexual vulnerability.

I could now look at a man in the street, say, or better yet a man at another table in a restaurant, and pick up unmistakable signals of submission from him.

"He'd be a good subject for domination," I'd say to myself, watching how a stranger conducted the business of ordering a meal. I realized I was reading mostly his relationship with objects, and that there were hints of subservience in the way a man touches a wineglass.

Again, this knowledge troubled me. Did I even want a skill like that? It struck me, brooding over it up in Coxsackie, that the weird rituals of S-M had filtered into my waking world. That wasn't supposed to be part of the bargain. I was supposed to have been inoculated against all contagion. What were my slaves to me, except a meal ticket?

It was only slowly, over the succeeding year, that I accepted this as part of the turf. I have even become a little proud of it. A dominatrix is not afraid of her own desire. I began, inevitably, to mythologize myself and my role in the sessions. If I was getting some emotional charge out of these transactions, so be it.

And it worked the other way, too. If I could bring something out of my professional life into my private one, that was okay, too.

I have become convinced, for example, that every woman in America can learn something from the elaborate rituals of S-M. To a certain degree—and every woman will recognize this truth—all men need to be trained sexually. The male animal is terrified of the female sexual organ and of the female orgasm.

"There's nothing there!" the little boy in him shrieks, "it's all inside!" Mystery! Darkness! The Unexplored Interior!

Sexual training is what S-M is all about. Domination is exaggerated sexuality, but it still has definite correlation to simple, straight-ahead missionary sex of the most vanilla kind. A woman can learn certain guiding principles from female domination. She can learn how to tell a man what to do in bed.

I'm not suggesting that every woman walk in off the street to sign up at a local S-M parlor. For one thing, anyone who thinks being a dominatrix consists of screaming at a man until his knees give way is going to be all wrong for it. This is not amateur hour.

But I do believe that all women should investigate the techniques and rituals of female domination. It should be one dialect in the language of love. Just as long as you don't start charging for it.

My Dearest Mistress,

I can't believe it, snowing again. No matter. But it shouldn't stop me from driving in. I am already on fire and looking forward to lighting a fire in you.

I nearly wrote to you last night, but I didn't have much to say, only what I was I thinking as I stood naked before the mirror, caressing my erection and feeling wonderful. Not just what I was thinking—I said it out loud, too. It sounded so good.

"Tomorrow Mistress Sonya will be flogging me." A trite, simple statement, but encompassing so much.

This morning I feel much more eloquent. I woke a few hours ago, still erect, with visions of beauty before me. Contrasting visions, the gentle beauty of your breasts—silky smooth, round, soft and firm at the same time, luscious, with their delicate pink tips— and the wicked beauty of the lash, long black sensual thongs.

How they both excite me just now. It is hard to maintain control, but I must to fully appreciate the hours of pleasure before me.

You might think that I am longing to be with you right now, but I am not. I want to relish the hours of preparation and waiting. The drive in, parking, knowing that I am near and it is going to happen very soon. Then walking to your door and entering into bliss.

Each time we have met it has been better than the last. I feel we are building a beautiful relationship, giving and taking, fulfilling each other.

But I do sometimes wonder if you are fully committed. Do you hold back? You cannot doubt my dedication to pleasing you, I am your slave, your toy. I long to feel that my body is important to you, that you look forward to using it to express your dominance.

I am not dedicated to pain per se. I know that I cannot take it when the setting is crude. It is pain administered by beauty that I adore. It is your breasts and your lash swinging as one. It is the thought of a beautiful dominant woman enjoying herself.

I am longing to see you. Let us devote ourselves to pleasures expressed by the lash.

Your eager slave,
G.

A little traveling music, please.

My work takes me places. Not always interesting places, but travel is travel. Sometimes, though, the perks are swell.

I spent the months of August and September one year in Milan and the countryside of Tuscany. My Milanese client installed me in his villa and then seemed to forget about me for a little while. I gloried in the heat and fragrance of the late summer. I was fed and taken care of by a short, dumpy cook who spoke no English. It was like a dream.

Other clients have imported me to other places, all over the country. San Francisco for two weeks at the Mark. Los Angeles, at a crumbling compound in Pacific Palisades that I was afraid would slide down the bluffs onto the Pacific Coast Highway in the middle of the night.

On the opposite end of the spectrum, I once went on an all-expenses-paid vacation, courtesy of a client. Sounds great, you think? That's the good news. The bad news is that it was an all-expenses-paid vacation to Oklahoma City.

Oklahoma City is not for the faint of heart. The average New Yorker, for example, flying into the airport and seeing the place set out on the plains, frying in the flat pan of the prairie, is likely to feel a slight twinge of existential nausea.

At least this one did, when I accepted the assignment ("Your mission, should you choose to accept it...") to join a client of mine in his home town.

I remember reading somewhere that the early American settlers, having crossed the Mississippi, went a little insane when they were confronted with the vast expanse of the plains. There was just nothing in the cluttered, claustrophobic European mentality to help them deal with this much empty space.

I could sympathize with them. Oklahoma City filled a little of that vast space of the plains, but it was like a pomegranate seed set down on an aircraft carrier.

Mark, my client, was the kind of genial middle-class boob that towns like this produce in such copious supply. He had a braying laugh, while at the same time, the Look registered in his eyes like a haunting.

I think he knew he was a fool, and he knew that everyone else knew, and that redeemed him a little because it made him sad. Anyhow, he made a lot of money compressing grass clippings into seed pellets to feed to chickens.

"Then I take the chicken shit, and I fertilize my sod farms with it. You get it? The grass feeds the chickens, and the chickens fertilize the grass!" Hee-haw.

He was divorced. One reason he and his wife divorced is that she could not see his need to be dominated as anything else but sick.

I think in the short run submissives make good husbands. You can send them trotting off to the store for a pack of gum and they won't object. Then the routine of their need settles in and it begins to drive their mates stark raving crazy.

One of the things Mark wanted to do, as a matter of fact, was to show me off to his wife. He wanted to take me all around, to his country club, to church. For once, I was actually serving the function they advertise in the Yellow Pages. I was Mark's escort.

He also wanted to string several sessions together over a three-day weekend. This was slightly problematic, because Mark was a whipping boy. Our time together consisted of grueling work with the crop, knout, quoit and bull-whip.

After each session, his ass and back would be terribly inflamed. I never drew blood; I always make it a practice of stopping short of that extreme. But after our first session in Oklahoma City, a short hour after he brought me home from the airport, I could not believe we were going to do this all over again the next day.

"I think you ought to let it rest," I said, as his back puffed up into welts. "We can do something else tomorrow."

"No, really," he insisted. "I'll be ready for you."

And indeed he was. I was astonished that he could still sit or walk or move at all after our second session, but he did better than that. He took me out to a Saturday night barbecue at his club. A wince of pain would cross his features occasionally, but otherwise he was his usual loud, obnoxious self. Although he had the bad luck to have a lot friends who were back slappers.

I played his mystery woman. He introduced me only as "Sonya." My look—I was wearing my sly little Thierry Mugler suit—caused some raised eyebrows, standing out amid all the lime-green prints and pleated skirts.

Church was going to be his crowning touch, since the former Mrs. Mark was going to be there. She turned out to be washed-out and brittle-looking, the kind of woman for whom the adjective "pretty" becomes a curse as they grow older.

She seemed confused and revulsed when Mark introduced me. He had gone out of his way. This wasn't really his congregation at all, and his presence there—and especially mine— was disturbing to her.

"I hate this," I whispered to him through clenched teeth as we edged into the pew. My old imaginary Jew upbringing made me loathe Christian services with a passion. It was a Pentecostal church. "I'm going to leave."

Mark caught my arm and whispered a request to me. I sighed. It was no skin off my nose, so when I rose to leave I slapped his face twice, very hard. The blows rang out above the polite murmur of the congregation like mini peals of doom. Every head in the place swiveled (except maybe the head of Mark's ex, who was looking determinedly at the floor) as I walked back down the aisle.

I have to admit I enjoyed it.

Dear Mistress Sonya,

It was very brief but our little chat has certainly brightened up a really dismal day.

Not that I have been depressed. I've been leading a very tranquil existence. Too tranquil. Pleasant enough but lacking fire. As always, your elegant, lady-like tones have stirred the embers into a very satisfying glow of anticipation. The fire is to come.

I have enjoyed thought of you in the last few weeks and relived our times together. It is the only way I get aroused these days. But for some reason I have refrained from calling you.

Today, when you were not on my mind, suddenly without warning I knew I had to call you. Strange, I was not thinking of the lash. I just had the desire to call you and to see you. Naturally, as we talked, and since, these other thoughts are very much with me. I feel so much more positive after I speak to you. I look forward to life with much more zest.

Probably that deep desire to sense beauty is always affecting me even when I am not conscious of it. When I know that it will be expressed within a few days my whole being is uplifted. It feels so good.

I am leaving to see you on Sunday. I look at myself, touch myself, and picture the scene to come. Those glorious moments when time stands still and I am truly living.

Oh, I am not tranquil now. The fires are really burning—as I hope my body will be on Sunday. How I long to stand proudly before you and be allowed to be the means by which you express your superiority and inner beauty.

Beauty and the lash, how I adore them. Please use me without restraint. I long to feel that I reach deep inside you to satisfy that wonderful part of you, the ultimate woman.

Your eager slave,
G.

Fetishism is a male phenomenon. That's the theory, anyway, laid down mostly by people who spend all their time safe and sound in the groves of academe.

The shrinks and behaviorists who have studied it say that fetishism is some sort of displaced phallus worship, that the shoe—or the women's dress, the latex suit, the enema nozzle—is a substitute for the prick. That's why women don't come down with it.

Women have a different sexual organization, these theorists say. The female of the species doesn't get her ya-yas off on boot-licking, cross-dressing, bondage, or any of the other myriad forms of male sexual strangeness. It's a guy thing. We gals wouldn't understand.

Nonsense, I say. The professors obviously haven't seen the lesbian sex clubs of San Francisco, or hung around the West Village during Gay Pride celebrations. The girls are learning to do it for themselves.

I see men almost exclusively. That's the whole idea, female domination of the male. But I made an exception once, one of those exceptions that proves the rule. As I think about it today it still gives me a chill.

It happened after my business was well established, during a particularly busy spell when I had been seeing one client after another, one blithering case of need walking in the door as another walked out.

The voice on the phone was different. His name was Charles, he said, and right away I noticed that he didn't have the tentativeness in his speech that was the aural equivalent of the Look. He asked me briskly, almost brusquely, about myself, at the same time fending off my questions smoothly.

He wanted to know if I ever saw couples.

Normally a red flag goes up at this. It's not that rare of a request. There are more things on heaven and earth, Horatio, than are dreamt of in your philosophy, and one of them is the existence of certain sexually predatory couples in the late 20th century western world.

These people are vicious and single-minded, out for their own kinks and their own kinks only. Other people are only tools for their bent imaginings and elaborate rituals. I knew the type well. They inhabited the edges of the downtown club scene, feeding off of it. They are usually spoiled rich kids from Europe, impossibly jaded and arrogant.

I pity any innocent who falls within their clutches. I remember a story a girlfriend told me, about a night of what she thought was going to be innocent sex that almost killed her.

"Gloria" met a couple of chunks of floating Euro-flotsam in a club. They all liked each other, Gloria, the man and the woman. The male of the couple was cute and nicely put together. The female downright beautiful. My girlfriend has been know to go both ways—although never, I hasten to add, with me.

A few drinks, some torrid touch-dancing, the three of them together on the small dancefloor of Au Bar. How about a threesome tonight? Gloria liked that it was the woman, not the man, who had suggested it.

Everything was sweetness and light until they had her tied up on the big bed in their hotel room. Then it was like some-body flicking a switch. They ceased to treat Gloria as a human being. She would talk, say something, and they would ignore her.

The male began to do unspeakable things to her body. Really horrible things, of which anal rape was the most pleasant. It went on for two hours. The woman sat there the whole time, watching bright-eyed. Doing the occasional line of coke and giggling.

The male stopped just short of disfiguration.

But mentally, perhaps, the experience was more brutally disfiguring than Gloria knew at the time. I could see she was still shaken telling me about it months later.

"I didn't know there were people like that in the world," she said to me.

I didn't know whether Charles, the voice on the phone, was a person like that, but why should I have even bothered to find out? I had plenty of clients. I had so many calls I had the luxury of choice. If there was any whiff of weirdness about any of them, the receiver slammed back into its cradle and they were out of my life forever.

But something stopped me from hanging up on Charles. Maybe I was bored. The endless parade of clients coming through my apartment was making me think that the circus should get a few new acts.

"Do you work with couples?"

"How do you mean?"

"My wife would like to experience domination," Charles said.

"I see," I said. "What would your role be?"

"I would be there."

"Participating?"

"Watching."

Male sexuality is a wonderful thing, is it not? I knew there were a lot of men who enjoyed watching their wives make it with strangers. "Pork," it's called in the trade, where it's not judged or condemned, just exploited. Hey, whatever slops your sow.

I had requests for pork before, and I always turned them down. But like I said, I was bored. I told Charles to bring his wife over for an interview. If I liked what I saw, and I could be absolutely sure that she wasn't being forced or manipulated into anything, we could perhaps set up a session.

I was pleasantly surprised. Charles was a handsome, winning 45-year-old with longish black hair and a relaxed manner. He resembled the actor Robert Klein, although he had the slightly crapulous look of a quondam drunk. His wife Andrea was a petite, flame-haired woman of about the same age, with the kind of slim body I had always admired.

By the confident, intelligent way she carried herself, I was immediately convinced that no one was bullying this woman into anything. She was merely sexually curious. Her husband had been to a "domina" before, she said, and they often used bondage and light whipping in their sex-play.

Actually, I was a bit intimidated by them. They seemed so happy, so well-adjusted and well-off. I could see that I was merely one stop along a path of sexual investigation that they had embarked upon. They were very loving to each other and did not really admit me into the intimate pas de deux of their relationship.

So be it. If I was a little envious of them, and a little jealous of her slim, athletic body, that would merely add a little tang to the proceedings. I sat Charles down in a chair facing my corner "office."

"Take your clothes off," I told Andrea.

For the first time she seemed to get a little meek. "My panties?"

"Everything."

As I left the room, I heard him gently mock her, "My panties?" She whispered back a laugh.

I went into my dressing closet to twist my head on straight. I put on a peplum-styled jacket and matching mini, both made out of some strange synthetic material that was a leather-spandex hybrid. The very latest thing in S-M couture. The jacket had a mandarin collar and laced down the front, and it fit my body as well as anything that slim bitch in the other room ever wore.

I put on some extra long black gloves and five-inch patent pumps and checked my look in the mirror. As I was dressing, I was psyching myself into a mind-frame of stone coldness. I tightened my face into a mask. I wanted to come out of there looking like the dominatrix of someone's dreams.

There were two soft gasps when I returned to them, so I knew that I had succeeded. Charles remained seated in the chair, but his eyes were glittering. I decided to ignore him and play to her exclusively.

She was pretty stunning naked. Her breasts were small, with bright, lip-red nipples. She had that creamy complexion most redheads can boast of, but unlike most, her skin was freckle-less. The vee of her crotch was red-haired, so I knew she was either a natural or went to the trouble of dying that, too.

"All right," I said to her. "I am going to walk you through this very slowly. I will tell you exactly what I am going to do before I do anything. If you aren't comfortable with any step or you want to quit, I want you to shake your head vigorously. Stop, or quit, just shake your head. Okay?"

"Sure," Andrea said, and again the meekness crept into her voice. It seemed deliberate, though. If there was such a thing as knowing meekness, Andrea exhibited it. It enraged me a little bit, her being in control even of her weakness.

It made me want to hurt her.

irst I am going to take away your mobility," I told Andrea, "and then I am going to take away your senses, one by one."

She licked her lips and nodded. This woman is too good to be true, I thought. Even her tongue is slim.

I opened a pair of fur-lined handcuffs that my friend Alex had given me as a joke when I told him about my new career as a dominatrix. They were lavish, ridiculous things, but actually quite perfect for use here. I snapped them around Andrea's wrists.

"Are you okay with this, Andrea?" Charles asked.

"Sure," Andrea said, looking straight at me. I lowered the silver chain that hung from the middle of the ceiling.

"I'm going to attach this hook to your cuffs," I told her, doing so at the same time. "Later on, I'm going to raise you onto your tippy-toes. I won't hang you off the ground. I just want your body stretched out."

I took out an elastic blindfold mask. As I raised my hands to fit it over her head our gaze locked. "Now I'm going to take away your sense of sight." Then I lowered it over her lovely green eyes. Contacts, I thought, tightening it. They had to be contacts. Eyes that green didn't exist in nature.

Next I took out a ball gag, a small, orange-red plastic object the size and shape of a ping-pong ball attached to a leather strap.

"I'm going to take away your ability to respond with words," I said. "Remember, if you need to stop, just shake your head, hard." I fitted the ball gag into her mouth.

"Next, I'm going to remove your sense of hearing," I said. I put a pair of paraffin ear plugs into her ears. She would still be able to hear me, but the sounds of the world would be muffled and indistinct.

She was effectively closed down as a human being. Her five senses were curtailed, all except smell and touch. She stood naked in front of me, her hands manacled in front of her, her head slightly bowed.

I tried to imagine her world. She had to trust me, a stranger she had met only a few minutes previous. She was blind. Her sense of hearing was almost gone, and the sounds in the apartment had become thick and turgid. She couldn't cry out if she wanted to. She was closed inside the world of her thoughts, and the world of her skin. Those two things were all that existed for her.

I leaned forward and put my face next to her ear. The scent of her hair was fresh and slightly flowery. "I'm going to raise your hands above your head." She nodded.

I stepped back and began to crank the chain skyward.

I glanced over at Charles. I had fully expected him to be sitting there with his pants unzipped, working his dink, and it surprised me at how relieved I was that he wasn't. He was sitting slightly forward in the chair, his gaze on the bound form of his wife. There was a thin mustache of sweat on his upper lip.

The chain slowly pulled Andrea's arms up above her head, and as her body stretched out it was like a flower opening. All the muscles smoothed from beneath her skin, and the full contour of her breasts asserted itself. Her back arched gracefully as her wrists rose, and finally she was poised, her toes curved like a ballerina's, her body fully extended.

I heard a small moan from Charles, but I ignored him. I leaned forward again and spoke into Andrea's ear.

"I'm going to apply a soft lash to your back and your ass," I said. "I am going to start very slow and soft. Remember to shake your head if you want to stop or change anything."

I chose a short, kid-skin crop with flayed ends. First I merely let it fall across the arch of her ass, but she flinched and tensed even at that. I caressed her skin with it, letting her get used to how it felt. Then I tried a few experimental strokes, light slaps really, laying them across the cream-white small of her back, then dropping down to her ass.

Her skin reddened immediately. I told myself to go easy, that I could raise a welt without even meaning to. I strode around to Andrea's front and began to flick at her breasts. Her nipples were already hard. Long pink striations from the whip crisscrossed her breasts and belly. There was a light sheen of perspiration between her tits.

I leaned into her, feeling her breath as it escaped from nostrils. "I'm going to insert a probe inside you, inside your vagina and your anus."

She moaned as it entered her, and she rose imperceptibly higher on her toes, arching her ass out, resisting the plug.

"Charles, I want you to come over here," I said. I didn't look at him to see if he obeyed, but I heard his boots as they clumped across the floor.

"Kneel down," I said. "Put your face into your wife's cunt."

I had no idea of the sexual dynamic between the two. For all I knew, he had not gone down on her for years. I leaned over and told Andrea that she would soon feel her husband's tongue on her clit.

Charles had a little trouble getting around the butterfly harness of the dildo, but he finally moved it partially to one side and was able to cram his face into wife's vulva. I stepped back and took a heavy knout-style whip from where it was pegged to the wall.

"If you want me to stop, just shake your head," I told Andrea again. Then I stepped back and applied the thick black leather to her backside.

As with the lambskin crop, I started slow. The whip snaked around her thin, size-4 ribcage like a snake. It snapped against her breasts and withdrew. I stroked her again and her body surged against her husband's face. Again. Again.

Andrea rose on her toes and seemed to climb up Charles's body. She wrapped her legs around his face and crushed him into her cunt as the lash came down again and again. With each stroke she would buck forward and smear her thighs across on Charles's lips.

After six strokes with the heavy whip she was ready. Despite the ball gag, Andrea gave a low, guttural growl. Her whole frame began to shake convulsively, and her hips slammed against Charles so hard that she knocked him backwards onto his ass. Her body drooped forward as she sagged from the chain, making no effort to keep her balance with her toes. Her thighs clenched and reclenched spasmodically.

I let her down gently by cranking the chain. She curled to the floor like a scarf trailed on the ground, quivering there as another climax passed through her body. Her husband crawled over to hold her.

There were massive red welts across her back, and I thought perhaps I had used her too roughly. I hadn't meant to grab for the heavy whip. It was too stiff to use on delicate skin like hers, and I rarely used it all except on the most toughened hides of veteran whipping boys, then only when they asked for it.

Charles removed her gag and her blindfold and her earplugs. I gave him the allen wrench that opened the cuffs, and he got her out of those, too. I could tell he was shaken by the whole experience.

She wept a little, and I left them alone together and went off to change out of my costume.

Dear Mistress,

Been trained in bondage, nipple & penis torture, foot & body worship, sensual teasing, enemas, dildo training, smothering, humiliation, obedience, and discipline.
Am here to be used and abused for your pleasure.

Thank you,
slave james

Walking out onto Park Avenue after a session, wearing my leather and heels, I found a street screamer blocking my path. "Surrender to Christ," she commanded, "or burn in hell forever."

Excuse me, but are those my only options? I'll take door number three.

Margate made me, T.S. Eliot says in *The Wasteland*, a poem written under the influence of a nervous breakdown. Well, Coxsackie made me. A nervous breakdown made me. A failed marriage made me.

Joanie and Fred dying made me. Bony fingers pawing at my Carter underpants. The Garment District. Biology. Depression. The way men treat women. Amphetamine.

The question is, now that I was made, what was I? The Christian screamers knew what I was. In their cosmology, I was evil, a scarlet lady, an unrepentant sinner.

I didn't believe them, of course, but I wondered myself. What exactly is a dominatrix? What function does she serve in the social mix? I was a cog in what machine?

It's curious that the feminists who get so much mileage flogging male use of pornography studiously avoid the whole issue of female domination. It is a round peg too hard to fit into the square pigeonhole of their analysis. They'll talk about female submissives, about *The Story of O* and *120 Days in Sodom*, but the other side of the coin is totally unexamined. Which is funny, because for every professional female "submissive" there are hundreds of dominatrices.

Am I an exploited woman? By their lights I am. I remember thinking, after Abe Shrader's buyer ripped me off for a blowjob way back when in the Garment District, that I would get even with the whole prick-addled gender of men. "If they are going to fuck me, I am going to fuck them."

Those who see the world as a conspiracy of men against women would make a lot out of the fact that dominatrices are actually at their slave's beck and call. It's not really female domination, they would say, it's only "play" domination. The truth is a lot less black and white than that. I am in control. I am manipulating rich white males, forcing a cash transfer to a member of a less privileged class, namely myself.

The feminists would point to all this and say, "See? Her mind has been twisted by the patriarchal attitudes of the society she lives in."

Maybe so, but I think that lets me off the hook a little too easily. I have an immediate, knee-jerk rejection of being made into a victim. I have made my own bed, sisters, and now allow me to lie in it. You're the ones who make such a big deal out of freedom of choice. Or does that only apply to abortion?

There are, of course, other elements in society that would condemn what I do, but these I find even harder to take seriously. I wonder what would happen if I wandered into a Roman Catholic confessional?

Forgive me, father, for I have sinned, and sinned, and sinned. Is that an altar boy you have in there with you or are you just glad to see me?

H.L. Mencken used to say that a Puritan is someone who is bothered by the knowledge that somewhere, somehow, someone was having a good time. But what do Puritans have to do with someone taking pleasure in being given a bad time?

It's all right, I want to tell Pat Robertson, Donald Wildmon, Cardinal O'Connor and the rest of the dead-from-the-waist-down pricks who want to perch on our bedsteads. Sex isn't supposed to be fun? I'll show you some folks who don't have any fun at all at sex. They're my clients, and for them, sex is pure hell, just like it's supposed to be.

William S. Burroughs says an old drag queen gave him a philosophy of life once. "And I've never been able to forget it," Burroughs would drawl. The world is broken up into the pricks and the johnsons. The pricks are the ones who are always intent on fucking with you, sticking their nose in your business, interfering and being busybodies. Johnsons are people who know enough not to argue or to judge. They take care of their own shit and leave everyone else alone.

The Cardinal O'Connors of the world, the Popes and the Pat Robertsons and the Ed Meeses, are all pricks. One day the johnsons are just going to get fed up with them, rise up as one and accomplish a ritual bloodletting. Some day a real rain is going to wash the scum off the streets.

All I know is that the ground was well prepared for him when Willie appeared to sow his seed. The making of a dominatrix. But I've told you I was born, not made, haven't I? Like a lot of people, I want to have it both ways.

"So how'd you get into this?" my neighbor down the hall, Jerry, once asked me.

I started to talk about needing the money, about how men used to come on to me all the time as submissives. Jerry shook his head.

"No, I mean how did you get to where you could do this, emotionally? Because you're really in the business of blowing people's minds."

I thought he was making a crack, but he was earnest. "That's what you do. They come to you, and they want you to blow their minds. It must get very tiring. How do you get up for it?"

I couldn't answer him then, but what comes to mind now is an evening I had, a week or so before Willie appeared.

I had gone out with Rudolf again. You don't have a relationship with Rudolf. You just accept the fact that you are part of a stable of girlfriends. If you did not part screaming at the top of your lungs at each other the previous time you went out, you can reasonably expect a call in a week, a month, a year... whenever he gets around to it.

We went to Cafe Tabac for dinner. There was Thierry Mugler, my favorite designer, sitting a couple of tables away.

And me with my father's old tuxedo jacket on, made by Franklin Simon 50 years ago. Rudolf knew I would be thrilled to meet him, and he brought me over. Dianne Brill came in then, looking great and 50 pounds thinner than she had the last time I saw her. The bitch.

"Hi, baby," Brill purred to Rudolf. Kiss, kiss.

"You're beautiful," she said to me.

"You're too kind," I answered.

"Did you and Dianne ever get together and play concentration camp?" I asked Rudolf when Brill had clumped away. Dianne is a nice Jewish girl from Florida.

"She doesn't have your sense of humor," Rudolf said.

Later that evening, we went over to the West Side docks to make out, like a couple of kids. The former club king's face was flushed and ruddy. It was a characteristic of the man. It was easy to find him in a club crowd when he was drinking. You just had to look for the shining red beacon of his mug. Rudolf's red nose reigns, dear.

I didn't realize the effect a few drinks had on him. You can't imagine the frustration of giving expert head and having a cock stay soft as a maggot no matter what you do. Especially after having been forced to listen to what a great cocksman he had been recently, fucking all those ski-bunny girls in Aspen, all those drag queens in Rio.

Rudolf begged and pleaded to be allowed to fuck me up the ass. This was a constant element in our lovemaking.

"You can't even get it up," I yelled at him.

"I'd get it hard for that," he promised me.

"Sure, okay—you can fuck me up the ass. For one thousand dollars." Rudy was a tightwad, and I knew that would shut him up. It did.

After our West Side attempt at paradise by the dashboard light aborted, we went to his place for more drinks. In exchange for his lack of performance, Rudolf became unexpectedly tender. He actually tried to bring me off, clumsily and with what was finally an annoying sense of persistence. I faked an orgasm.

Later, I sat in his living room and listened to his snores coming from the bedroom. It was approaching noon. I felt inconsolably sad. There is nothing in the world quite as deadly as the sound of the birds on a morning when you've stayed up all night. I remembered it well from my amphetamine days. Like Muzak in hell.

I woke Rudolf and told him that I could not possibly go home dressed the way I was, my tits falling out of my jacket like two puppies trying to escape from their cage. He gave me a t-shirt and some gabardine pants to wear, and I caught a cab home.

The same glaring driver. He lies in wait for me outside Rudolf's, like a troll under a bridge. Or maybe they are all the same man, all the cab drivers I've ever had in Manhattan. Paranoia strikes deep.

When I went into the bathroom at home to wash up, I noticed an impossible odor coming from my body. Because of Joanie's relentless early toilet training, I am an obsessively clean person.

As soon as I took them off, I realized the stench was coming from the clothes that Rudolf had given me. I examined the pants. There was a caked-on ridge of chocolate-brown shit as big as my finger in the crotch seam, and several dried stains of semen inside the fly. I took a half-hour shower and washed myself with hibaclens to remove the stink from my skin.

The pants I threw down the garbage chute, holding them away from my body with a pair of kitchen tongs. After a moment of hesitation I tossed the tongs down the chute, too. I vowed it would be a long time before I gave that man another blowjob. No wonder he didn't wear underwear.

I have wasted my life, I thought, as I sat on the couch in my apartment, my skin still tingling from scrubbing. I must inject some form of honesty into my existence, I swore to myself, or I am doomed.

So this was the frame of mind that I took to the gallery opening where I met Willie. The faint stench of a dishonest life hung about me. Maybe the whole gabardine-pants incident represented some sort of last straw for me, because looking back I know I was ready to change.

It is difficult for me to claim honesty as a virtue of my profession, but in a strange way, I think it is.

Everything I had done previously led up to me becoming a dominatrix. I think resisting it, refusing it, would have been dishonest.

Of course, after Rudolf's shit-stained pants, maybe I was just ready to be impressed by Willie's fastidious personal hygiene.

It all has come full circle. I don't really know if dominatrices are made or born. Probably, as is the case with me, a little of both. It's just how I make my living now.

My family knows what I do. Some of them are embarrassed by it, and some of them are comfortable.

"Mommy is spinning in her grave," a sister who still lives in Coxsackie told me.

Maybe. But I don't think so. I have a picture of her, propped up against my wall in my apartment, a head shot from her Norman Norell days. Her eyes are cast down, like the Madonna in the Michelangelo's Pieta. She looks beautiful and serene.

There are times that I catch a glimpse of her in mid-session, as I snap my crop across a client's buttocks. Her photo is of great curiosity to my slaves. They all think it is strange I have a picture of my mother where I work. In a perverse way, I think it adds a little excitement to the proceedings for some of them.

Mommy, Mommy.

I don't have to wonder what a shrink would think about my having it propped up there. But that's okay. Some of my best clients are shrinks.

It's like the old joke. Doctor, says the guy on the couch, the memory of my mother is haunting me. I can't get her out of my head. I should have been a better son to her before she died. I can't sleep, I can't eat. Her face is always before me. What should I do?

I don't know, says the shrink. The fucking bitch is after me, too.

Yeah, we all know the bitch. She comes snarling out of our subconscious, out of our childhood, to squat on us and tell us we're no damn good. Some of us have got her worse than others, but we all have her to some degree.

My clients are the ones who have her worst of all. Sometimes I think I'm a great liberator. Other times I know I am merely sinking them deeper into their ruts. Most of the time I think what I do is not good or bad, not evil or redeeming. It just is.

But I know that my role in life, at least for now, is to play her. The eternal Slut-Mother. That's what I do for a living. I embody the bitch. The men who I do it for are so grateful afterwards that they sometimes cry.

So I was hoodwinked into it by two masterpiece Matisses, by a mother who wouldn't quit and a father who would, by a quirk of biology and by a pair of dirty gabardine pants. So what? All you can say about it—if you don't want to get up on that dangerous high horse—is that it's not morally good or morally bad. It just is.

But nobody does this forever. Where do I go from here? It's a question that has drifted across my mind more than a few nights, as I've lain awake, waiting for sleep to come. The answer that I've come up with may surprise you, but then again, it may not. It surprises me.

But what the hell, it may be worth a laugh. Through all this, through all the phone calls and the appointments and the casual whoring, I have held on to a cracked sort of dream. I am sometimes baffled by it, because it seems so alien to who I am now.

The dream I have is terribly middle-of-the-road and boring. I want a home. I don't care if it's an Upper West Side duplex or a Victorian with a white picket fence around it in Great Neck—it's the idea of the a home that's important, not its particulars.

I want a husband. Yes, a husband. A real mate-for-life this time, not a fellow inmate in the loony bin. I want us to be strong and good and funny together like people are in the movies. I want to struggle through things together the way couples are supposed to do, without rancor and with love.

It's silly, isn't it? For me to still hold on to this dream, faded and dusty like an old keepsake. I try to actually imagine myself with a husband. I wouldn't know what to do with him. But I know that deep in me somewhere there is a place that holds fast to that fantasy.

In my fantasy, I am always in this vague green space—a park? a yard?—and the two of us are lounging around, taking our ease, contented with each other. It's a beautiful spring day, and I am happy.

In my mind, there's an overwhelming feeling of security and certainty to this image. I don't know if it will ever actually become real, or if it's just a holdover from some childish dream.

But in another sense, I truly believe in it. I know he and I will be together forever. As long as he doesn't ask me to spank him.

Sonya,

Mommy Dearest
Mistress Mine
Deal with me as you wish!
You are going to anyway.
I hope I please you.

R.